"There is no better way to [connect with other hu]man beings than to engage you[r heart]. [In this] compilation of human connection, women share their heart with tears, joy, fear, sorrow, hope and learning with you! Hear what God has done and what He continues to do when the stakes are at their highest. I know you know what this means, because you have experienced it too."

Stephanie Cole
Wife, Mother, Jesus Freak
Atlanta, GA

"This book is filled with inspirational true-life stories of hope that will ignite or reignite your faith in God and His miraculous plans for you. God always shows up right on time, in His timing and this book is a wonderful testament to that and so much more."

Aurea McGarry
Emmy-Award-Winning TV Show Host
Atlanta, GA

"We all have a life story that is as unique as an individual snowflake. What I love about each and every one of the *women* featured in this book, is that they had the courage to *tell* their story. What I love about this *book*, is that readers will not only learn something from each story – they will feel *inspired*. I am truly blessed to know many of these women personally.   My prayer for each and every reader is that you will also find the strength and courage to *embrace* your own story and share it."

Becky Gregory
Mother, Friend, Crazy-Fun Woman
Atlanta, GA

"Here's a book where ordinary women are transparent and gives the general public a clear view of how they dealt with the ***Even So*** when "bad things are happening to good people". Too often, women are encouraged to keep silent and bear the burden of that silence.   ***Even So*** will give so many women, and even men, the courage to speak up, speak out and keep speaking."

Freda Doxey
MA, RMHC
Atlanta, GA

"So much of Christian life is focused around the blessings in our faith walk. What few will risk talking about are the sufferings that many, if not all, Christians experience. ***Even So*** is a «real life» journal of how when bad things happen to good people, there is still a God that is present and His grace is sufficient. ***Even So*** is a MUST READ. No matter where you are in your journey, it will encourage you that God is enough!"

Mike Ennis
Campus Pastor
Springville, AL

"This book is a powerful glimpse of God's grace in our struggle. You can see how God never leaves our side, even in our darkest moment. He is forever faithful. He holds all of our unknowns."

Tracy Goodwin
Author of *Unstoppable God*
Spring Hill, TN

"How does one get over the feeling of being deceived, abandoned or disappointed? Questions often impact and shape a life's story. These stories tell about life and offer encouragement for all of us to trust in a power greater than ourselves. These circumstances didn't destroy these women, but instead, ignited them to move closer to the true source of life."

Terence Chatmon
Husband, Father and Author of *Do Your Children Believe?*
Atlanta, GA

"I know these strong women personally and I know their stories. These are stories of faith and strength in the face of adversity. We can all learn from these real life examples that these people have lived out in their own lives. See these circumstances through their eyes, live in their shoes a little while, but most of all, let a little of their faith and strength rub off on you as you read their stories."

Hilmer Hintz
Husband, Father, Follower of Jesus
Ankeny, IA

"Life is difficult. Scripture reminds us that we live on Satan's territory and until Christ returns to vanquish him, we will. For reasons we cannot fathom, God requires some people to walk through almost unbelievable trials. The stories of these women who did that will inspire you and strengthen you in your own journey! May God bless each of them!"

Bob Bruton
Co-Founder of the Gypsy Project
Richmond, VA

"This collection of heart-moving stories reveal the deep pain and struggle many women have experienced. Story after story is a testimony of God's faithfulness, healing power, and unending love for us. This will bring hope and encouragement to anyone who seeks healing, peace and freedom."

Thomas Otley
Pastor, Jesus House of Prayer
Atlanta, GA

"It is my joy to endorse this inspiring book co-authored by several devout women of faith who have journeyed through a season of difficult challenges in their lives. I am personally acquainted with several of the ladies and know about the tests and trials they have endured. The challenges have come in many forms, but all have resulted in seasons of confusion, questions, and severe tests of faith. Each story is a testimony of God's faithfulness in the midst of the storm. These stories will bring encouragement and renewed hope to anyone who feels overwhelmed with the difficulties of life."

Doug Carter
Senior Vice President, Equip
Atlanta, GA

"Even So inspires us to look at life and love differently, with eyes of faith and hope, despite the challenges life may bring."

Claire Dees
Executive Director, Spectrum Autism Support Group
Suwanee, GA

"Thank you to all of these remarkable women for "bearing your souls", and for sharing your stories of tragedy, pain and suffering; yet you have come through it all in VICTORY as you've learned to put your hope and trust in the Lord. Your stories show great courage, strength and tenacity that can only come through living each day in His presence.

In reading your amazing stories, I am reminded of this Scripture...

Psalm 91:1-2 which reads "He that dwelleth in the secret place of the most High shall abide under the shadow of the Almighty. I will say of the Lord, He is my refuge and my fortress; my God; in Him will I trust."

In reading these stories, no matter what you're going through, I believe you will be encouraged and realize that you are not alone! You too can be an overcomer!!"

Pat Bruton
Co-Founder of the Gypsy Project
Richmond, VA

"In a day of social media perfectionism, whether it's a staged photo with just the right filter or the perfect phrase to reflect "perfect" lives, this book reflects the real lives of women following their Savior. Their real lives have been messy, filled with hurt and definitely not social media worthy, but they have a Hope! His name is Jesus, He has reached into their lives and healed their bodies, relationships, minds and renewed them because He is the God of Hope."

Kimberly Burks
Wife, Mother, Grandmother and Women's Ministry Leader
Atlanta, GA

"With amazing authenticity, but with hope for a better day, the stories that are shared are guaranteed to relate and encourage every reader. I'm convinced you will love each account and be glad this book came into your possession."

RD Saunders
Vice President of Advancement, Equip
Atlanta, GA

EVEN SO

STORIES of HOPE and ENCOURAGEMENT

FOURTEEN WOMEN'S STORIES *COMPILED BY*

SHARON BURCHAM

dustjacket

Published by Dust Jacket Press
Even So: Stories of Hope and Encouragement / Sharon Burcham

ISBN: 978-1-947671-70-6

Dust Jacket Press
P.O. Box 721243
Oklahoma City, OK 73172
www.dustjacket.com

Dust Jacket logos are registered trademarks of Dust Jacket Press, Inc.

Cover & interior design: D.E. West / ZAQ Designs - Dust Jacket Creative Services

Printed in the United States of America

www.dustjacket.com

TABLE OF CONTENTS

FOREWORD
by Sharon Burcham

It's not unusual for me to wake up in the middle of the night. I had it happen one night in early November 2017. I immediately had the thought that there should be a book written by women, for women, to encourage women who were going through a difficult time and feeling alone. Each chapter would be written by a different woman who would tell her story, and I was supposed to steward this project. So, after the thought came into my head, I dismissed it, turned on some worship music and tried to get back to sleep. I told no one about my thoughts because certainly it wasn't anything I was going to entertain.

A few weeks later the same thing happened again. This time I changed tactics and had a little talk with God explaining that I didn't have time to steward a book. I reminded Him that I was a reader and not a writer! I further "explained to God" (can you imagine such a thing?) that I don't have the expertise to accomplish this crazy idea that was suddenly dropped into my heart. Surely, I was mistaken that this idea was inspired from Him. I once again put on some worship music and attempted to get back to sleep.

The third time I woke up in the middle of the night, I just got up and started writing down names of extraordinary women that I knew had a story to tell. I quit volleying with God and started praying, and asking Him to bring other women into this project that He knew needed to be involved. I told God that if this was from Him, He needed to direct me to a good publisher....and he did! Dust Jacket said yes immediately to being our publisher, and they have been incredibly encouraging. I started speaking to the possible book contributors and asking them to pray if they wanted to share their story. There were a few ladies that decided it was not the right time for them to participate; while others felt the conviction immediately to be a part of it. There are some new friends along the way that God provided for their stories to be included too. No one has a chapter in **Even So** by accident. It has all been intentional. God's intention.

To all the beautiful ladies that wrote a chapter and shared your story and your heart: thank you for saying yes - thank you for your transparency - thank you for trusting me to steward this in a way that is honoring to God and to you. I love you all and am grateful for this trip we all took together!

To the reader holding this in your hands right now: I trust these words will bless you, encourage you and give you hope. We pray that you will share it with your friends and those that need to know that **Even So** things are challenging, just keep putting one foot in front of the other. God always has a plan.

Sharon Burcham
Jeremiah 29:11

TRANSFORMATION:
Turning Tragedy into Triumph

AMY MODGLIN

When you read my story, I want you to see God's greatness. Instead of looking at the sadness and hurt, I want you to look at how God knew me and loved me before I knew and loved Him. Please, do not feel bad for me, but rather focus on how much God loves me, as well as the grace and mercy He has shown me—and the redemption story which is playing out in my life. If you already know the Lord, I hope you will rejoice with me in His greatness. If you do not know the Lord as your personal Savior, my prayer is that you will read the stories of the incredible women in this book, and you will be curious about what your life would be like if you had a Father/daughter relationship with Him. If you know the Lord but you have experienced some things that have made you question your faith, I pray that you will be inspired by God's faithfulness in my story. I pray that you will see that despite the suffering I have faced, **Even So**, my love for the Lord never waivers. I pray that you will see God's pleasure lived out in my story.

James 1:2-3 (NIV) says, "Consider it pure joy, my brothers and sisters, whenever you face trials of many kinds, because you know that the testing of your faith produces perseverance." If I had read this verse twenty-five years ago, I would have dismissed it. Today, it has become my "life" verse. It reminds me that God has chosen me for this journey I am on. Every single trial gives me the strength and ability to get through whatever my next battle is.

An important detail for you to know is I did not know God personally until I was well into adulthood. The only exposure I had to church as a child was with a friend of mine. I will admit, I went more for the escape from home than for the experience of church. I always believed there was a God, and I used to pray to God all the time, but I did not realize at that point what it was like to have a loving relationship with Him. Today, I am trying to give you something I never had when I was younger; someone to tell me about God and encourage me to seek Him.

My childhood years were traumatic. I often wondered if there really was a God. I questioned if He really existed, and if He was real, I wondered why He would let me go through some of the things I went through. I remember being told there was no such thing as God, and I was mocked when

I would mention Him. Due to some of the things that were happening around me, I often thought that maybe there was no God.

At the age of thirteen, my life took a dramatic turn when I was taken out of a bad situation at home. It was a chaotic and terrifying time for me. The next five years were spent moving around from foster homes to shelters to group homes. I lived in over 25 different places, including some time on the streets. I went to nineteen different schools from 8th grade to 12th grade. Those were the worst years of my life. It was hard to make friends when I did not know if I would be going back to the same foster home at the end of the school day. I did not know how to form healthy relationships, so I just pushed people away. I have never felt so lonely and hopeless as I did during that time in my life.

There were never any expectations for me or for my future. For the majority of my life, I was told I was worthless. Once I entered the state system, it only got worse. All I ever heard was I would be nothing, I would fail at everything, I would never get married, nor ever own a home, and I would never have a successful job. The sad thing is I believed everything I heard. I thought I was nothing. I did not believe in myself. I did not fight for anything. I just accepted things the way they were. Little did I know that God was showing me how to overcome and persevere, so I could share my story to impact others in the future.

I was called "a victim" and I was treated like "a victim" for so many years that when I would get in trouble, it was just brushed off because I was a "victim." When I talked about becoming something in the future, I was told that victims like me never make it in the world. I think it is because of being treated like a victim for so long that I refused to adopt the victim mentality.

My feelings of unworthiness were further cultivated by the environments I was in and by the things that were happening in my life. At this point in my life, I often share the symbolism of a black trash bag. When I finally got a chance to go back to my house, escorted by two police officers, it was a moment of intense emotion. My emotions were compounded when they handed me a black trash bag and told me to fill it with "everything you need." What does a thirteen-year-old need? At this point I did not know if I was ever coming back, so I grabbed some clothes, a few personal mementos and my hairbrush.

Over the next several years, I moved around many times. Sometimes I would stay somewhere for a day, or even just a few hours. No matter where I went, I toted around my black trash bag with "everything I needed." It did not take long for the bag to start ripping and for my things to get stolen. I tied knots in the bag to keep things from falling out. It was so demeaning to show up at the next place with my ripped trash bag. The most unfortunate thing about this part of my story is that so many adults saw me during this time. Not only was no one paying attention, but no one thought of the implications for me in having to carry around that black trash bag.

Finally, a staff member at one of my group homes brought me a legitimate bag to carry my stuff from place to place. I am so grateful she took the time to pay attention and do this for me. It gave me a sliver of dignity when I showed up at the next doorstep. You do not put things you value in a trash bag—you put trash. I was treated like trash. I believed I was trash. Therefore, I lived like I was trash.

When I was sixteen, things were at rock bottom. My life was going nowhere. I had already attempted to take my own life twice. I was spending time with other kids who were a bad influence on me. I was heading down the road everyone had predicted for me. That was until God used another staff member to speak four simple, yet profound words to me:

I BELIEVE IN YOU.

I had no idea what this meant. I asked a lot of questions and discovered that I did not have to end up like everyone expected me to. I could make decisions to change the trajectory of my life. I was literally at the fork in the road where I could make the decision to continue to live my life as a statistic, or I could choose to defy the odds. I had straddled the line for so long, more often leaning towards a destructive path and less often towards the redemption path. Hearing "I believe in you" empowered me to make the decision to turn away from the bad decisions and away from being who I was predicted to be. Psalm 71:20 reads "Though you have made me see troubles, many and bitter, you will restore my life again; from the depths of the earth you will again bring me up." I can look back now and see how God was working in my life, even though I had not yet chosen to trust Him.

My life before 30, was a disaster. I made bad decisions. I had no respect for myself and ended up in many unhealthy relationships and dangerous situations. After 30, it changed in a profound way! That is because I entered an eternal relationship with my Heavenly Father. I am not proud of the person I used to be, but I have been completely transformed since I have given my life to Christ. I no longer worry about being unworthy or unloved. I know that God loves me unconditionally. He loves me on the days I live out my life purpose and on the days that I fall short. Most importantly, I know He will never give up on me and He will never abandon me. He loves me despite the hurt and the shame, despite all the bad decisions I have made, and despite all the times I have failed. He ordered every step of my life. He knit me together in the most unique way. I am exactly how He wants me to be. He knew I would suffer, overcome, and make a feeble attempt to use my story to help others. After all, God knows our plans. When we pray for His will to be done and not ours, miraculous things start to happen!

I am so incredibly grateful to the Lord for giving me the trials and tribulations that He has. If I had not had the struggles I did early on, I would not have the fortitude and the grit to be able to face today's challenges. Tragedy has become my triumph, and it has transformed my life. With God I am ready to face everything. For me it is a privilege to have suffered so much, so I can have tangible stories that show God's greatness and love.

Life with Christ gives you hope, but does not take away the challenges. **Even So**, God chooses special people to go through special circumstances. About ten years ago I got sick. I was diagnosed with two conditions that would completely change my life. One of my diagnoses was discovered during an infertility workup. Yes, I wrote that word. Infertility. It is awful. My husband and I went through years of unsuccessful infertility treatment. It's another blessing to thank God for. As it turns out the doctors later said that I would have probably died during childbirth. Although the pain of not being a mother will always be with me, so will the miracle that He knew I would not make it through. *Blessings do not always appear in the way we hope and pray.*

In 2011, my health took another decline. It was then my doctor told me it would be a miracle if I lived five more years. For the first year I was angry, scared, and worried about dying every day. Today I realize what a blessing every single day is. Facing my own mortality has completely changed my perspective on life. I decided I was not going to live towards what my doctors told me, but that I would put my head down and lean on the Great Physician. People who know me best say I make it look easy. Well the credit does not go to me. All the glory goes to God. He obviously wants me to do something significant in my life and whatever it is, I am ready to live it out.

God chose me for another battle. Eight years ago, I started to lose my hearing. By the time I acknowledged it, I already needed hearing aids. It started to become extremely difficult to hear people in loud environments, like restaurants, so I started to pay attention to people's lips. My doctors told me I would never lose all my hearing, but the Lord told me to learn to read lips. This is yet another thing for which I am grateful. About two years ago I did completely lose my ability to hear, and I am now clinically deaf. I thank God I learned how to read lips, because that is the only way I can verbally communicate with the world. It is terrifying and lonely to live in a completely silent world. Rather than focusing on what I can no longer hear, I focus on the only voice I can hear: God's voice. This is such a blessing. People pray every day in hopes to hear God's voice, and it is the only one I can hear.

I have often been asked how I have been able to endure so much. The answer is simple: it is all God. I believe God has gifted me with tragedy that is beyond human understanding. I am grateful that God prepared me for the future. I thank

God every day for the incredible gifts He has given me, things like a positive attitude, emotional strength, and resilience. It is so easy to concentrate on all the bad things in life. I could focus on all of the things I have "lost," but what I have gained is crucial to why I am still here seven years after my doctor said I had five. My circumstances do not define me. What defines me is my faith and obedience to the Lord. God is so good to me. I am insanely blessed.

I realize that every single day of life is a gift from God. I never want to take this for granted like I used to do. Every morning, when I realize I am awake, the first thing I do is thank Him for giving me the opportunity to face another day. The next thing I do is to visualize a wrapped gift. Every day the gift looks different. I imagine the color and texture of the ribbon and the paper. In my mind I unwrap that present with anxious anticipation. When I open the box, I realize that I have opened the greatest gift; another day of life, another opportunity to make a difference in the life of another person. Doing this helps me keep things in perspective. It keeps me focused on my blessings and keeps me thanking God for this gift.

I believe that we sometimes must come to the end of ourselves before we realize we cannot do it alone. Things start to change when we understand we are not humanly capable of turning our lives around. We may try to ask others for help, only to realize that we need something more. What I realized was that I needed Jesus. This relationship is what has changed me. I would not be here today to share my story without Jesus' grace, mercy and love.

I know my joy comes from the Lord. I know that He has brought me through everything, so He can prepare me for something significant in the future. Every day I thank God for every single trial, every hurt and every tragedy. There is not a single detail of my life where I would want a "do over." I know that God has orchestrated every detail of my life. I know that I am a stronger, more resilient woman because of this journey. Everything I have worked through has made me stronger in my faith and better equipped to be used by Him. It has allowed me the blessing of being able to find strength when I am brought to my knees. It allows me to see life through a different lens, one that I was never able to see before. It has made me able to recognize His hands all over my life. It has made me walk through life more confidently. I know that in His eyes I am exactly how He wants me to be. Doctors can tell me I am going to die in five years, but I know I will have eternal life in Heaven. That brings me a joy like nothing else in life can. Each day of my life I focus on living in the joy I have for the miracles I have seen in my life.

Only by going through so much have I come to depend on the Lord like I do. There is no trial, no heartache, no failure, no disappointment, and no pain that would ever alter my love for Him. Nothing can rock me enough to make my faith waiver. When I think of what He has suffered for me, there is nothing I would not suffer for Him. He will never give up on me, and He will never stop loving me unconditionally. I will also never give up on Him, and I will continue to embrace every step He chooses for me to take. ***Even So***, I will only love Him more every day. I could have gotten *bitter*, but instead I have chosen to get *better*.

For my story, all the glory goes to God. God's gift to me is my life. My gift to Him is how I live it out every day. It is a gift I accept with great humility.

"What is more, I consider everything a loss because of the surpassing worth of knowing Christ Jesus my Lord, for whose sake I have lost all things. I consider them garbage, that I may gain Christ and be found in him, not having a righteousness of my own that comes from the law, but that which through faith in Christ – the righteousness that comes from God on the basis of faith" (Phil 3:8-9, NIV).

ALL THE WAY

ANGELA POWELL SMITH

More than a decade ago, I discovered a VHS tape of my mother singing a song that I have titled "All The Way." Although I have searched through her bags of sheet music, I still have not found it. The words of the song are "All the way, all the way, all the way, I just wanna go, all the way. Sometimes up, sometimes down, almost leveled to the ground. I just wanna go, all the way. If I stumble while I'm toiling, don't be angry, just let me stand. I am a witness that I will go all the way." This song exemplifies a theme in my life which is to go "all the way." So, I decided to name this chapter, *All The Way*.

My sister and I grew up in a single-parent household. My mom loaded her car with members of our church, along with my sister and me, and then we headed to Johnsontown (Lenox Square/ Buckhead) every Sunday for church and to visit my grandmother. This appeared to be Mom's number one priority. My mother, an anointed pianist and gospel singer, helped me experience the presence, love, and power of God on different levels. Not only did I learn about God from Mother and the Bible and hymns, but there were also deacons, ushers, and older women in the church who I believe put feet to their faith. I saw widows who were confident. They walked with their heads held high and willingly bowed down on their knees and prayed during devotional service. One of the widow's prayer had a rhythm to it as she quoted Proverbs 3:5-6. The widows were not intimidated by the aging process and death had no sting. Death seemed to be viewed *simply* as a part of life. I rarely heard them mention Satan's name. It was as if he had no power or authority.

As I reflect on my childhood, high school years, and college years, I see this pattern of going *all the way.* I believe that my burning bush experience manifested itself after graduating from Talladega College (Alabama). This experience shifted my mind-set, leaving me with a different kind of thirst. That thirst led me to increasing my time in Sunday school, weekly Bible studies, and reading Christian self-help books. This phase of singleness was orchestrated by God. As I begin this new chapter in my life, please know that God is still carrying me right now. I am just relaxing in His arms until I catch my second wind.

By early adulthood, I believed in the power of fasting and praying, so I prayed for a husband. God heard my prayer and then He blessed me with a wonderful husband and best friend, Randy. We were married thirty plus years ago. We raised three sons, two joined the military, following in their father's footprints. My sons have families of their own that include four beautiful grandchildren. Our marriage was far from perfect. We experienced sunshine, partly cloudy skies, as well as storms. Nevertheless, we knew the power of prayer. My husband was convinced that God answered my prayers, so he nicknamed me "The Bride of Jesus." We were in the season of pressing our way, self-actualizing, fulfilling our life goals, and enjoying the fruits of our labor. Randy decided that it was time to make a change, so we packed up and moved to Forsyth County, Georgia. Why Forsyth? Well, that's a chapter for another book.

I was in the final phase of completing my doctorate while working full time. Meanwhile, Randy, a retired Sgt. Major, disabled Veteran, and Certified Bikram Yoga Instructor landed the job of his dreams with the Department of State/Bureau of Consular Affairs and Technology as the South Central Regional ISSO. He was so happy because his job site was downtown ATL. This fulfilled his childhood dream, to work in downtown Atlanta and wear business suits every day (As a boy, he admired how the Civil Rights Leaders wore suits). My husband was skilled in information systems and cyber-security. I think he was a GENIUS! He loved staying ahead of security vulnerabilities. Randy monitored the passport networks as soon as he woke up (at the crack of dawn), during the day, and throughout the night. The agencies that he monitored maintained high ratings. He often repeated this motto that he learned in elementary school, "Good, better, best, never let it rest until your good is better, and your better is best." People who knew Randy, or sat and spoke with him briefly, could see and hear his giftedness.

I recall during my doctoral dissertation defense (Argosy University), my laptop malfunctioned, and suddenly the power-point presentation disappeared. Can you believe that? Technical difficulty!!! I determined that it was nobody, but Satan behind the scene, trying to derail me again. Before I knew it, I screamed R-A-N-D-Y, and he jumped up from his seat in the audience, did his magic with the computers and placed me back on the *yellow brick road.* That's my man, Randy, always to the rescue. This was his nature, to help anyone that he perceived needed his assistance, and with a smile.

Randy and I were like macaroni and cheese. Usually, when you saw one, you saw the other. Natalie Cole, in one of her greatest hits, called it "Inseparable." Randy called it "giving each other a heartbeat." On the weekend, we fried fish on Friday evenings, followed by singing solos and duets. He loved music. On Saturdays, he arose early, fixed his coffee and sat on the front porch with his two cellphones and a laptop. By 7 a.m., he would call for me to join him and I would, however, not without grumbling as I fixed my tea. Randy often used this time to reflect on our life together and assess how well we had worked as a team. We discussed future plans, my career as a counselor, and then he shifted to "If something happens to me........". I never liked that part of our Saturday morning reflections. After our reflection time, he headed to yoga. Yoga provided temporary relief for his back. By afternoon, we would prepare meals, play several games of pool and shift to ping pong or watch television. On Sunday mornings, I was off to church, and he was off to teach Yoga and check on the properties. We prepared Sunday meals together, watched a little television and then called it a day.

Randy loved hosting our annual family and friends reunion at our home (Labor Day weekend). This started after his mom died—since her birthday was early September. He was the backyard "DJ" and everyone loved his music. We cooked the food and opened our "Smith Home of Comfort." That's how he described our home. For us, life was good. We were slaying life's giants and living each day to the fullest.

The Saturday after our last cookout, Randy woke up early and started his day. An hour or so later, I left home for a board meeting (LPCA), followed by a noon wedding for my Godson's sister. Randy and I discussed attending the wedding together a week earlier, but I noticed he had not arrived yet. I said to myself, "I am going to get him when I get home!" Then I said, "Maybe something came up that needed his attention." After having a busy week and a wonderful time at the wedding, I came home tired and drained. I set the house alarm and said to myself, "I am going to tell him a thing or two when he gets home." I recall receiving a call from my granddaughters, after speaking with them, I laid across the bed. My alarm clock woke me up for church the next morning. I then noticed that I was still dressed in wedding attire, and the alarm was still armed.

My internal alarm alerted me that something was wrong. I sensed my heart rate going up. I started praying and pacing, trying to calm down. I said, "What am I going to do, Lord?" I heard the Holy Spirit say, "Stick with your routine." I worked out to calm down, then went to CCC (Christ Community Church—Cumming) at 9 a.m. While in church, I kept taking deep breaths and asking God to help me. Shortly after my arrival, I received a cordial text from my niece, "Good morning, Auntie!" I responded back. The next text from her stated, "Where's Uncle Randy? He didn't show up for yoga. We are outside waiting for him to open the studio. That's not like him." As my heart dropped, Pastor Jason's sermon sounded as if he was speaking directly to me. The topic was "Scriptural Truths for Dealing with Pressure." Interestingly, he stated something like, "Sometimes in life you can feel so much pressure until you think you can't take it, but you have got to hold on to God." The more I listened, the more it became clear that the Holy Spirit was getting a message to me. At end of service, I left church, went home, changed clothes and put on one of Randy's military polo shirts—"Georgia National Guard- Defending Freedom." I recall being focused on "I've got to find my husband." I began to carve out strategies to locate him. By now, I was not feeling fearful or panicky. I called his cell phone several times and called all the hospitals in the metro area over and over. I visited the VA hospital in Decatur. I called his oldest brother, but there was no answer. I headed to Atlanta to search there. After searching as much as I knew how, I went to my uncle's house and told them, "Randy is missing."

As I drove home, I started interviewing my sons for their last conversations with their father, but I still did not tell them what was going on. The second time I called them, I said, "Your dad is missing." I returned home, still no truck and no return call from Randy. I called the hospitals again and now the jails. I drove back to Atlanta, spoke to my brother-in-law and my cousin with APD, and headed to the 106 property with the keys. God would not allow my keys to work. After the firemen opened the window, we helped my cousin climb in the window. Once she cleared, I started climbing in the window, she yelled, "Angela don't come in." I ran to the front door where my brother-in-law stood. My cousin called the homicide division. I remember wailing uncontrollably and screaming, "NOOOOOO!" I must have blanked out because when I came to, I was on the ground and my clothes were dirty. The unthinkable had happened. My husband was found senselessly murdered on September 11, 2016.

This property was once a flower shop, "Flowers by Vine-yard." It was the place where Randy and I first met—the place where our life together started and ended. Around 1:45 a.m., I left our property after his body was removed. I drove myself home in a daze, listening to a gospel soundtrack by Sheki-nah Glory, entitled, "Yes." My mind drifted back to one of our Saturday morning conversations when Randy stated, "If anything ever happens to me, I need you to give the eulogy because you are the only one who really knows me and the boys will listen to you." Without hesitation, I honored my husband's request. I delivered the eulogy. I believe The Holy Spirit suited me up in God's Armor because it seemed as if I was in a trance-like state. He had a full military funeral with honors, and so many family members, friends, co-workers, classmates, yoga students and church family attended the ser-vice. I thought I would collapse as I watched Randy's flag-covered casket being removed from the hearse at the gravesite. Then suddenly, I received a hug from one of the WNBA chaplains. Where did she come from? She lives in Texas. *Even So*, that hug stabilized me. It was the very "touch" I needed from God. As the soldiers folded the flag, preparing to give it to me, I turned to look for my sons. And there they were. Two of the three of them were dressed in their military uniforms—saluting their father's casket, with tears streaming down their faces. I held my grandchildren as I tried to get my mind wrapped around the fact that my marriage of thirty-three years had ended. That day, all I know is that God kept and comforted me with His "wind beneath my wings."

Can you imagine that? My life with Randy is over—F-O-R-E-V-E-R!!!!! My sons supported me in granting permission for "The First 48" (Season 17/E1- Honor Code) to show the episode so that we could find out what in the world happened to him. I still find myself thinking, did this really happen? Randy is dead!! Never again will I hear him say, "Hey Sugar" when he enters the house.

Moreover, the youth who confessed to two of his close friends that he killed my husband—sharing detailed information that only the homicide detectives knew—was released from jail. In January 2018, a jury found him "not-guilty"—even though the evidence stared them in their faces. That too, is a chapter for another book. My message to Satan is this, "You didn't win because I have the victory in Christ Jesus."

Because I know that life has mixtures of good-bad, ups-downs, bitter-sweet, pain-pleasure, smooth roads, potholes, and detours, I don't have to ask God "Why?" ***Even So***, here are a few ingredients for my recipe for going "All The Way."

A) A bowl of "spiritual fitness" means to maintain an intimate relationship with the Trinity (Father, Son and Holy Spirit)

B) Mix in a cup of personal praise and worship throughout the week

C) Stir in journaling— (a grief journal is a separate journal)

D) Pour in remembrance of God's goodness

E) Add wholesome Christian activities to use the gifts and talents that God has placed inside me

E) Toss in crying and resting—without apology

F) Fold in my daily bread (manna from heaven) for this day ONLY. I don't mix in worrying about the past or the future

I will lift my eyes beyond the hills to The God of Abraham, Isaac and Jacob, knowing that He is My Help, My Strength, He is whatever I need Him to be, NOW and Forever more. This is my truth! I believe the essence of Psalm 139 that God formed and knitted me together in my mother's womb . . . that I am fearfully and wonderfully made. Moreover, Jeremiah 29:11 tells me that God has a custom-made blueprint for my life, a plan for me to prosper, a harm-proof plan that is full of hope. Because, I embrace His will as my truth, I can stand and face each day.

Isaiah 43 reminds me that the waters of life will not drown me, and even when life heats up, I will not be burned, nor will I smell like smoke. God is my Redeemer. Therefore; I fear not.

Even So, I am going ALL THE WAY! Won't you join me?

THE FLIGHT

CAROLINE HICKMAN

I felt the water begin to pool at my feet. I looked down to see hair in the drain. My hair. Enough hair to have clogged the drain. I began to go numb; I barely made it out of the shower before I collapsed onto the floor. I was broken. My breathing began to go faster, and I felt tears streaming down my face. I could hear the shower running in the background, and somebody was banging on the door. My mom ran in and picked me up from the mess that was on the floor. I stayed in bed for the rest of the day, curled up in a ball, thinking about that wad of hair. I felt the empty patches on my head. In that moment I was a sinking ship, going further and further into the abyss, with nobody around to hear my screams. I cried out, asking God where He went.

Cancer. The word nobody, especially a fourteen-year-old girl wants to hear. I, Caroline Hickman, had just turned fourteen. I was full of hope and wonder for the newest chapter of my life, high school. I was curious as to what it would mean to me. Would it be "the best four years of my life" as some proclaim or just another school I attended with bland people who wouldn't leave an impact on me?

The summer before my freshman year is when it all started. One day, after an early morning field hockey practice, my knee began hurting. It felt like someone was stabbing me repeatedly. Later that week, my father took me to the emergency room to get it checked. They believed I had slightly strained my knee. Of course, just for that they decided to give me a giant knee brace and crutches.

Later that summer, my other knee flared up out of nowhere. They both were so swollen and painful that I could hardly even move in my bed. Slowly, my appetite started to go. I could hardly keep down a protein shake, let alone food. My mom and I ran from doctor to doctor, trying to figure out what was wrong with me. I had blood test after blood test, with no answers for me. Finally, one doctor pronounced that it had to be Lyme disease. So he put me on an herbal oil medication in an attempt to help my condition. After a month of that and no change, my mother looked at my blood test results and found an unusually high result in one of my counts.

December 16, 2015, I was admitted to the hospital. I weighed eighty-three pounds, and my hemoglobin (the protein in my red blood cells) was 5.7. A normal person's is 12 or higher. They said it was a miracle I was still functioning. And on December 18, 2015, my entire world came crashing down around me. My mother and father told me that I had cancer. Everything stopped the moment they said that word. My chest felt like it had been hit with a ton of bricks. My ears tuned out everything, and I could hear my blood rushing and my heart pounding as I sat there in shock. I could see my mom's mouth moving, but I didn't hear a word she was saying. When I snapped back into reality, I found out my type of cancer was called Acute Lymphoblastic Leukemia, also known as ALL.

Later that day I walked out of my room into the bleak halls of the oncology floor. As I walked the halls, the inspirational posters on the greyish blue walls seemed more depressing than anything. The air smelled like a mix of medicine and fear from parents, including mine, who didn't know what was going to happen to their children. The halls were empty, except for the occasional nurse. Most kids weren't allowed outside of their rooms because of their weak immune systems. As I walked laps around the floor for what seemed like hours, I realized that this was my new reality.

You always hear about cancer survivors and their stories, but you never expect to be one and have your own story to tell. I was angry. In my mind, God had betrayed me. It took me a while to realize that God was not doing this to me, but the Devil was. God knew I could handle this even when I didn't. "For I know the plans I have for you," declares the Lord, "plans to prosper you and not to harm you, plans to give you hope and a future" (Jeremiah 29:11). We spent the next few days starting chemo and going over treatment protocol. On Christmas Eve, my grandparents stayed with me overnight in the hospital. I didn't want my parents there; I wanted my three sisters to have as normal of a Christmas as possible. Christmas morning my grandmother was following the attending doctor around, asking for my discharge. She kept going until finally he caved and came to my room to give me the all clear. At 12:15 I was allowed to go home. It was a Christmas miracle. Little did I know that was God's way of telling me, "I've got you, Caroline."

The first month was the most intense and most painful. I was put on a high dose of steroids called prednisone—that made me eat everything in the house to get my weight back up, while also killing the cancer cells. I was so small that anyone who gave me a hug was scared they were going to break me. While gaining weight was great, it also meant getting sick a lot. Chemo was so intense that month that I could hardly function. My little sisters brought me food when I was too weak to get out of bed. I was mentally and physically drained, and then my hair started to fall out.

I decided I had to take control of what was going to happen, before it did. I decided that before all of my long, luscious locks fell out from the chemo, I would give myself a buzz cut. My hairdresser, who I've known since I was three, agreed to come to my house for this emotional moment. Very limited family and friends were allowed to be there for this sensitive occasion. I sat in the middle of the room as everyone watched in silence as the hair hit the floor. I let the tears silently roll down my face as I lost a piece of myself. I felt like I was losing my identity—a teenage girl without hair was not going to go unnoticed. However, I knew it was better than watching it come out in patches and having no control over it. I silently prayed for peace, as I felt my hair being removed from my head, hoping that God would hear my prayer. I tried to make the best of the situation and had a "Hat Party" later that night with all my close friends. We all wore the most ridiculous hats, hoping to lighten the mood through the night.

Right before I had left the hospital, I got something called a chemo port. It's a small disk with a jelly substance in the middle that is put under the skin right below your shoulder. It connects to one of your main arteries in your neck. The port makes it easier to receive blood and chemotherapy. Basically it's like a constant IV, so you don't have to get new ones every time you need something. At the end of the first month, I needed two units of blood transfused because the chemo had lowered my hemoglobin. Each unit was two hours to transfuse. Those two were the first of many that I would need throughout the next two and a half years. The first time I received blood, I had an intense reaction. Actually, it was the worst reaction you could have after getting a port. Blood clots. Not just one either. I had blood clots all up and down my entire left arm. There were so many that my whole arm was swollen. I went into the dreaded ICU for three nights. Those three nights were a very low point for me. I was given an expensive drip bag of medicine that would hopefully break the clots up. It did nothing. They decided to give me another bag full and hoped it would work. If it didn't, I would need a new port in the other shoulder, which nobody wanted. I will never forget those three nights. It was loud, cold, and I felt disgusting.

I had countless ultra sounds with the disgusting gel that they wouldn't totally wipe off, leaving me sticky and unable to shower. I didn't have an actual bathroom. I had a cabinet that when you opened it, a toilet swiveled into the middle of the room. My amazing father only had a chair to sleep in when spending the night with me. I was so bitter and irritated those three days. "I already have cancer, why does it have to be harder than it already is?" I thought to myself. Thankfully, the second bag of medicine broke up the clots. However, now I would need to be on blood thinner shots twice a day until the port was removed. My mom learned how to administer them from a nurse and I was allowed to leave.

Many people began to visit me, telling me I was in their thoughts and prayers. Telling me I was so brave and courageous. But courage is simply grace under pressure, and I was just doing what I had to do. "Joshua said to them, 'Do not be afraid; do not be discouraged. Be strong and courageous. This is what the Lord will do to all the enemies you are going to fight'" (Joshua 10:25).

The next few months were excruciating and harsh on my body as well as my mental state. I was throwing up constantly from all the chemotherapy my tiny body was receiving. I would get dizzy easily and everything would go black when I stood up. I went to the clinic once a week for chemo, sometimes more if I needed blood. This continued for a year, and every single time my wonderful mother took me. We would sit back there for hours and she would never leave my side. Which always amazed me because she is a stay-at-home mom for my three sisters and me. I know how hard it was for my sisters, especially my two younger siblings, with Mom being gone all the time with me. I also know that they understood and just wanted to get me back to normal. I tried my best to never show how scared I was to my parents and sisters, because I knew they were already terrified. I know they were also trying to do the same thing to protect me. My siblings were truly amazing during this whole time. They were constantly asking me if I needed anything and trying to put a smile on my face when I needed it. The youngest sister, Rachel, would bring me anything I needed to my room and was constantly asking what she could do. Sara, the second to youngest and the creative one, would always make me little crafts to try to make me feel better. Hannah, the oldest one, would always try to relate and give me advice, as well as, keep me updated with what was going on at the high school because I was no longer allowed to attend.

When April rolled around, I had to go into the hospital a total of six times to receive high-dose chemotherapy. The average time patients were in the hospital for treatment was five days, four nights. Your blood had to have a certain level of chemo in it before you were allowed to leave. One way to clear it was to drink tons of water and sweat out the chemo. So, that's what I did. Every time I was in the hospital I drank gallons of water and walked ten miles around the hospital floor loop. Every hospital visit I was out within three days and two nights because I was determined to leave. Even So, when I was there I felt like God was speaking to me and telling me to help others. So, when the nurses asked if I would be comfortable talking to a girl who had just gotten diagnosed, I jumped on the chance.

Apparently, she wanted to talk to someone closer to her age. She ended up being in the room next to mine. I walked in the room to see a girl with brown, short hair. She looked up at me, smiled, and said, "Hi, I'm Kelly." Little did I know, later I would think of that girl like a little sister. I introduced myself to her parents and her older sister and sat down. She began asking questions, cracking a few jokes in between to lighten the mood. Her family was curious and had a few questions of their own. I stayed with them for hours, until I finished getting my chemo and had to go back to my room.

The next day I decided to show her how to tie a headscarf in case she ever wanted to tie one. We talked and got to know each other a little better and eventually exchanged phone numbers. Later that day, the social worker and I came up with an idea, a scarf tying session. I invited all the girls on the floor to the common room to learn how to tie a headscarf in cute, fun ways, should they ever want to wear one. The next six times I was in the hospital, I ended up talking to lots of recently diagnosed children and their families, answering questions and praying with them if they were religious. However, none of them got as close to me as Kelly.

The next few months were all the same. Treatment, schoolwork, sleep, repeat. It had become the new normal for me. My homeschool teachers would come to me daily so I could keep up with my work. I got used to being alone, because even though cancer isn't contagious, people are still nervous to come near you. I grew accustomed to the pity looks from strangers. All the months began to blur together. Going out in public was rare and very much appreciated by me. Going from being a social butterfly to being in isolation was an adaptation I was not prepared for.

Seven months later, I had adjusted to this new life of mine when I began to feel my I.T. bands in my legs getting tight. So, in October I started to go to Physical Therapy to try to loosen them up. After months and months of physical therapy with no results, my family and I decided it was time for a change. My mother found a new physical therapy place that specialized in I.T. bands. In order to get in though, you had to get X-rays of the area to make sure there was no underlying problem. So on February 21, 2017, my mother and I made an appointment to have the X-rays done and see the physical therapist. On that day, my entire world was shattered once again.

I had Avascular Necrosis (better known as AVN) in both of my hips as well as my right shoulder. Basically the steroids I had to take to kill the cancer cells had killed my femur heads as well. The steroids had cut off the blood supply to my femur heads and caused them to collapse, as well as my shoulder. The physical therapist described it as a square peg trying to fit in a round hole. My hips were now square and my sockets were still round and I—at age 16—would need a double hip replacement. My mother and I were in shock. We were just trying to get into a PT place, not get this news. Another piece of my identity was being stripped away. I was an athlete.

The next few months were dreadfully painful, especially the winter because of the arthritis that had developed in my hips. It eventually got to the point where I was immobile. I was so confused as to why God was testing me again. I had found my faith again and hadn't strayed. I trusted Him and realized that cancer was a part of His plan for me. So, why was

He testing me again? Then I realized that He wasn't testing me again, this was a part of the journey, and one I would overcome. "We are hard pressed on every side, but not crushed; perplexed, but not in despair; persecuted, but not abandoned; struck down, but not destroyed" (2 Corinthians 4:8).

Finally on April 13, 2018, I was cancer free! I felt a huge weight lifted off my shoulders. However, celebrating this major milestone was difficult because I was still in so much pain. It seemed like years before I could get my surgery, which was scheduled for June 20th. However, my hips ended up getting so bad that I wouldn't have been able to move if we prolonged it. So, the surgeon moved my surgery up to May 16, 2018.

I had another long road ahead of me after my surgery. It took weeks to be able to just get in bed on my own. I was required to use a walker and a cane, which usually ended up frustrating me. After weeks of physical therapy, I was allowed to walk on my own. I haven't taken a single step for granted since dealing with that awful experience. Ever since then I have only been experiencing life to the fullest. I am now enjoying my senior year and am an active member of my high school varsity field hockey team, which, I never thought I would have been able to do.

I haven't had the easiest life, and I am sure many others haven't as well. However, a caterpillar cannot be helped out of its cocoon. It must fight and believe it can emerge. Once it does, it is more beautiful than ever before. ***Even So***, God shaped and molded me while I was in that cocoon. He had never abandoned me. He just wanted to see how strong of a warrior I was, and in the end He got me through it. He gave me a new perspective on life and made me realize what I wanted to do in life. Yes, there were rough patches in my faith, but He always helped me see His reasoning, even if it took a while. They called me "Caroline Tough," but courage comes after you act.

THAT LITTLE VOICE

JANEL BROOKS

I knew I was different from the other kids when I was in elementary school. *Even So*, I didn't necessarily know how I was different; just that I was. When I got to middle school, it hit me: I was the "fat kid." All throughout school and growing up, I was that kid who was bigger than everyone else. I also started to develop some facial hair and other characteristics that were not typical of being a young woman. In middle school I was picked on and bullied a lot by my classmates.

Around that time, I fell and got a stress fracture in my foot. I had to wear a boot and limit my physical activity. When some of the boys found out what happened, they ridiculed me. "No wonder she got a stress fracture…she is the size of an elephant," they would say. I also heard a lot of hurtful things like "boom boom boom" when I passed by certain classmates.

Even 20-plus years later, I can still hear the mean words they used, and I can see the looks on their faces. By high school, I was hoping my parents were going to tell me I was part of some crazy medical experiment. I thought maybe they would tell me that all the extra weight was just a fat suit, sewn onto my naturally thin body. When that never happened, I had to come to the realization that I was actually that overweight and unhealthy. At first, I did nothing about it, hoping it would just go away on its own. That never happened either. By the time I got out of college in 2000 I was obese, had unwanted facial hair, no menstrual cycle, and I hated myself. This was not necessarily the way I wanted to start my adult life.

I knew I wanted it all, and for me, that meant a successful career and family. I also was pretty sure those things would not come at my current weight. There was a little voice deep down in my gut telling me to lose the weight. I didn't even know where to begin. I felt so alone, and I didn't think I was going to be able to get healthy. The voice stayed in my gut for a few months. Then I got up the courage to call my doctor's office to make an appointment for a physical, something I had been avoiding for years. My goal this time was to get help. It was time to try and lose this weight, because I felt that I owed it to myself. This seemed to me to be the first step in getting what I wanted out of my life.

At the doctor's office, I found out that I was 330 pounds. I was ashamed and embarrassed. But the doctor suspected that I might have Polycystic Ovarian Syndrome (PCOS), and he told me I needed an endocrinologist to make the diagnosis. I left that appointment with two things that would change my life in a way I could never imagine: a referral to an endocrinologist and a nutritionist referral.

My first appointment with the nutritionist was very eye-opening. During the first part of the appointment she was asking a lot of questions, and we had a conversation about my life, my food, and my movement. She asked me if I had ever been seen by an endocrinologist and been evaluated for PCOS. Thankfully, I could tell her that my appointment was a few weeks away.

She explained that PCOS is a hormone imbalance syndrome that affects the female reproductive organs. It also comes with symptoms of type 2 diabetes, hirsutism (excessive facial hair), the body makes too many male hormones, acne, excessive weight gain, heavy or no monthly cycles and the strong possibility of being unable to have children. It is also common to experience anxiety and depression. I learned that my body processes food differently. I never really had eaten horribly; I had always eaten a lot of vegetables and fruits. At the same time though, I was also eating a lot of "white things:" potatoes, pasta, bagels, white bread, and things like that. If I was insulin resistant, my body was not breaking down and metabolizing the food I was eating as it should. This was causing a feeling of hunger when I wasn't really hungry, leading to overeating and weight gain. She said I had all of the classic signs, and she was going to treat me as though I had it. My first goal nutritionally was to eat more fruits and vegetables and to come back in four weeks. That was it, and it seemed fairly doable to me.

When I went to the endocrinologist, they ran some tests and when I went back for the results, it was confirmed. I was diagnosed with PCOS. He put me on birth control pills to regulate my hormones and cycle. He also said the best way to manage PCOS was through my lifestyle. He explained that healthy eating and moving my body needed to be a part of managing this syndrome.

My second appointment with the nutritionist revealed that I had lost 10 pounds. For the first time in a very long time, I was proud of myself and excited to see what the future months would bring. She also explained how exercise would help me with this process. I started walking my dogs and then started an exercise DVD at home.

I continued to meet with the nutritionist every four weeks or so and most of the time I was down eight to 10 pounds. We would talk about different healthy foods and meal ideas I could try. I would explain my struggles within the process and she would give suggestions on how to overcome them. She was coaching me, she was educating me, and she BE-LIEVED in me. She believed in me when I didn't believe in myself. I worked with her for almost 2 years, and in that time, I lost 128 pounds.

You know who else believed in me? That little voice inside my gut. That voice led me to call my doctor, and it led me to my PCOS diagnosis, and to the nutritionist. Not just any nutritionist…to MINE. She has the PCOS knowledge and experience. She had the instinct to treat me as though I had it, even before the official diagnosis. Without all of that, I would not have been successful. That nagging gut instinct led me to a healthy life. Back then I did not realize what or who that nagging voice was. Throughout my journey, I realized it was God and my belief in His plan for me and for my future.

It has been roughly 18 years since I started my health and wellness journey. I have kept all of the weight off and become a fairly accomplished endurance athlete. I started moving my body with some home exercise DVD's and walking my dogs. Eventually the walking turned into running, which led to racing, which led me to a triathlon. To date, I have completed three Half Ironman races. I have also continued running races on a regular basis. I gained a belief in myself through the success of losing weight that led me to believe I can do anything I set my mind to. I have pushed my physical limits in ways I never could have imagined.

Remember how I wanted it all? I wanted a successful career and a family? Well, I have both. My husband and I have been married for over 10 years. He never knew me at 330 pounds, and I am glad for that, because I was not the strong independent woman I am now. I needed to start my journey and get healthy before meeting him. I needed to know myself and show myself what I was made of first. When we were dating we decided if we ever got married we would not have children. This was partly because of my PCOS, and also because I didn't want to go through the heartache of trying and potentially not being successful. When we did get married I stayed on birth control to help manage my PCOS. About two months later we received a surprise: we were pregnant! This seemed impossible, here I was with PCOS and on birth control, and suddenly pregnant. Once again that little voice in my gut was telling me this baby was meant to be. God knew all along I was meant to be a Mom. The other thing that gives me joy and fulfills my purpose is helping other people with their own health and wellness journey. I realize now this was all part of Gods' plan for me. I get to use my experiences and my knowledge to help others believe in themselves, just as my nutritionist believed in me all those years ago.

Our daughter recently turned 9 and she knows that when I was younger I was very unhealthy. When I was explaining the opportunity to write my story for this book, she said, "Mom, I am so glad you are who you are and you got healthy. Otherwise, I might not exist, or I might be a boy." It suddenly became even more clear to me; I had to go through this journey, and I had to get healthy not only for myself, but for others. I had to get healthy so I could share my story and believe that others can get healthy too. I was meant to be a good example for my daughter. That little voice inside my head was leading me down a path, and I had to trust that good things were going to come from it. When my daughter said those words to me, I knew she was the biggest reason of all.

Getting healthy and staying that way has been hard. It's been extremely, incredibly HARD. It's normally a daily struggle when it comes to what I eat. Most of the time I take it meal by meal. The biggest thing that helps is pre-planning. I plan my family's dinners a week in advance and base my grocery list off of that plan. Sunday afternoons are spent in the kitchen making our dinners. I also make a big salad every day for lunch and use an app to log my food and workouts every day, it helps me stay on track and keep the weight off.

Mentally I thought once the weight was off, my life would be perfect and I would love myself and my body. Well, it turns out I was wrong. There are some days I still see myself as the obese, unhealthy woman I once was. There are days when I am right back where I was all those years ago, slightly depressed with very low self-esteem. Part of the struggle with PCOS is treatment. The best thing to do is eat healthy foods and exercise. Sometimes that is not enough and some type of medication is needed. In 2016, I decided to go off the medication I was on. The voice in my gut told me it was a bad idea, but I did it anyway.

Within weeks of being off the medication the depression started. I remember one Sunday afternoon in April, my husband was working in the garage; our daughter was watching a movie, and I was sitting on the couch crying. There was no reason to cry – at least none that I could think of. The depression really took over that day, and it was crippling. I vividly remember thinking that if I were no longer here, no one would even notice or pay attention. That's what depression did to me. It made me feel so insignificant that it felt like my life did not matter to anyone. As soon as those thoughts entered my head, I heard that little voice in my gut again. It told me that I mattered and that I needed to get help. The very next day I called my doctor's office and explained what was going on. I made an appointment for a week later and got myself back on my medication. Once again, I let God lead me, and it was the right thing to do.

Throughout my journey I have met some incredible people. One thing I have realized about most of them is that they are unhappy with their weight. Weight is a common problem that many, many people struggle with. Sharing my story gives me the opportunity to let everyone know that they are not alone. If I can do this and be successful for so long, so can you. If I could learn to believe in myself, you can too. You are worth loving yourself for who and what you are. You are worth the hard work it takes to get healthy and stay healthy. Listen to the little voice in your head, and take the first step.

COMING BACK TO ME

KELLYE MULLINS

THE DECISION

It was the second day of withdrawal. I lay in my bed, sweating, crying, with cold chills, rubbing the skin off my legs and arms from my restless body and basically wanting to die. My stomach was rebelling almost as much as I had been during the last five years. How does one get here?

My 13-year-old son (the oldest of my two boys) kept checking on me. Every time I would open my eyes he would be there with "the look." The look that says, "I'm worried. I'm scared. Is she going to be okay? She's my mom." And when there would be a lucid moment for me, I wondered the same thing. I had two amazing sons and I wanted to be fully alive for them. In fact, they were a big factor in my decision to admit and end my addiction. I had put off withdrawal because it was all so unpleasant. There were times I felt incoherent.

My memory of the third day is foggy. I had been in bed 72 hours and I didn't know what day or what time it was—and I didn't care. I just wanted to feel better, and so far, that wasn't happening. I had had no food, only the Gatorade my son made me drink. I had not told him not to get help from anyone, but he knew that my parents did not know of my addiction, so the withdrawal process would have been a shock for them. I knew I would have to deal with that situation later.

When I made the decision to get sober, I never thought about my hair. In three days' time my waist-length hair was matted and snarled almost at my shoulders because of all the tossing and turning I had been doing in bed. I should have put it in a ponytail, but who thinks about that when you are looking at getting your life back? My appearance on day three was rough; but I didn't care. It was the least of my worries.

HOW DID I GET HERE?

For so many years I had experienced back pain issues. There was a season I did injections and they seemed to help for a while. But then the pain would come back with a vengeance. I started seeing a pain management doctor. The more medication they gave me, the more I took. The more I took, the more I needed . . . and the more the doctor prescribed for me.

I had been in two car accidents over the years and while neither of them was a major collision or was my fault, they resulted in significant back issues. Both times when I had been hit, my back was affected. I was somewhat relieved to discover pain clinics, but little did I know they would not be the answer to my pain. Instead, my problems were going to become worse. The last year of my addiction I was prescribed 50 mgs of Percocet and 30 mgs of Dilaudid. This was supposed to be a 30-day supply, but it only got me through 15 days. We have always heard that one thing leads to another, but we rarely believe it. Since I didn't have enough drugs to get me through a month, I had to find them elsewhere. I had a "so called friend" that introduced my longtime boyfriend and me to heroin. The first time we snorted it, we didn't feel anything. Then we were told we hadn't done it correctly . . . we should have been shooting it. So, that began. It seemed to work to alleviate the pain. In fact, I didn't have back pain. I didn't have any pain. I felt nothing.

As I fell deeper into addiction, taking the pain meds orally was replaced with using a needle. My boyfriend and I had promised one another we would never use a needle in our veins. Soon, that pledge had been broken. At this point he and I were not together. He had managed to get clean. As I was lying in my sweat and tears, I wondered how he had done it. What had he gone thru? Was it the same as me? I needed to talk with him. I was scared, but more determined than ever. I could do this. I knew I could. I hoped I could. I prayed I would.

MY YOUNGER SELF

When I was growing up, I had parents who loved me—and they still do. I am an only child and, even though my parents divorced when I was ten years old, as a kid my world was fairly normal. I rebelled and had some issues but nothing like drug addiction. Going back and forth from my parents was challenging and by this time both my mom and dad had remarried. My mom was strict, and my dad was not. My rebellion was dependent on who I was living with at the time. While I wasn't a fan of rules, in all those years I was never in trouble with the law nor did I abuse any substances. I tried things, but nothing became habit forming. I thought I was being smart, but I didn't see what my parents saw. I was reminded many times by them what would happen if I did such and such, and I thought, "What is their problem? It's my life, I know what I'm doing, and I'm not doing anything but living my life." I never put much stock in their concern.

They were right to have concern for me because of the company I kept and the places I went—and an attitude that was pervasive. Anyone would have thought that if I was going to have an addiction problem it would have been when I was younger—not a 30-something mother of two.

I grew up going to church, but I only went because I was made to go. It wasn't that I didn't believe in God, but there was not much of personal relationship with Him. When I was with my mom, I would go to church with them, and I would fit in while I was there. When I was with my friends, I was a different person. I remember one time after a particularly difficult situation, my mom asked me if I knew the difference between a chameleon and a lizard. I responded, "Yes. A chameleon changes color with their environment and a lizard stays the same. She asked me, "What are you?" I knew I was that chameleon. Then she asked, "What am I?" My response was, "A lizard, Mom. You are definitely a lizard."

ADDICTION

One of the first things an addict learns to do is to hide the addiction. The second thing you learn to do is be around people that are doing the same things as you are. It's easier that way. Then you are only having to pretend 50% of the time. There was no one except the people I used with that had any idea of my addiction. My parents did know that I went to a Pain Clinic to manage the back pain, but the amount prescribed was never discussed. There was a time that I was out of pills, and I called a girl I knew to see if she had any drugs I could buy from her. This individual didn't have anything to sell me, but she offered to make me a shot (of heroin). A friend that was not a drug user came with me. When we arrived at the house, we went into the bedroom where I was asked if what was in the spoon was the right color. I didn't know, and she didn't know, but we both assumed I would be fine. I do remember getting the shot and then stepping backwards and losing my balance. When I came to, my head was in my friend's lap and she was crying and rocking back and forth. She kept saying, "Please be okay. Please wake up." I was okay, but apparently, I overdosed. I could have died. I was so sick.

THE NEXT STEP

Laying there in my sweat and filth, I was scared—but I had come this far, and I wasn't turning back now. My former boyfriend had told me about Suboxone and how it helped him get sober and stay sober. Suboxone is an opiate blocker that is widely used to treat opiate addiction and withdrawal. Maybe that could help me. I needed to talk to a doctor.

I decided it was time to call my mom. I started the conversation by telling her I needed help. I was day 3 into detoxing and while I don't remember all of what I said, I know she didn't ask many questions. I was being as vague as possible about my use of drugs the past few years and what it had come to. When I was around family, they had no idea I was hiding in plain sight. Hanging up from her that day I felt shame, but I was also proud of the choice I had made to change my life. No turning back now. I had to get through one more day before seeing the doctor.

When Mom picked me up I was embarrassed, but it was okay. I was also relieved. I was clear headed and that hadn't happened in quite a while. She let me roll out the story as

I felt comfortable; we didn't do too much talking on the way to the doctor. On the way home my words came easier and as I shared, she cried. We sat at Chick Fil-A holding hands and crying. I told her what I thought I could handle telling and she could handle hearing. Being sober gave me a spark of hope that I hadn't felt in a very long time.

My priority has always been my boys; we did everything together. It had been just the three of us since their dad and I divorced. I didn't get up one day and just decide to become a junkie; but **Even So**, I became one. My boys are my life. I wanted to be there and be whole for them, as well as myself. You have to get sober for yourself. If I had continued down the path I was on, I surely would have lost my incredible sons and maybe my life. God had been good to me in spite of myself and my lack of regard for Him. Things were going to change. I had a new lease on my life, and I was going to make good use of it.

Most of my circle of friends changed; it had to. My attitude changed. My priorities changed. And I looked for ways to make a difference. It was a time of discovery for me. I was going to make a brand- new start. I can honestly say I was not tempted to go back to the drugs. Having been an addict for five years and doing it later in life—rather than in my developing years—was in my favor not to relapse.

After two and a half years of sobriety, I was offered the opportunity to work at a Sober Living program. I began to learn and understand about addiction. How it has no age limitation or gender. It is not a respecter of persons; anyone can become an addict. I realized too that in Scripture we know that Satan was an angel before he fell. He was the chief worshiper. Addiction is from the Devil.

TODAY

I have now graduated from Certified Addiction Counseling Training. It was an amazing experience that will allow me to help others when they find themselves in a similar situation as I did. I was so fortunate that I was able to withdraw the way I did at home. It's highly unusual—and not recommended. When I think about my oldest son putting a chair in my room and just watching over me for hours to make sure I continued breathing, I am humbled. He took my pulse every hour and wrote it down. The fear I put him through, I trust, will keep him aware of how easy it is to get entangled and how hard it is to walk away from an entanglement. While my youngest son didn't understand at the time what was going on, he does now, and we talk about it. There are no secrets in our home.

There were parts of my addiction I had not shared with my family until recently. I'm not proud of my addiction, but I am proud of the decision I made to end it. Today I'm in a good place; raising my boys and enjoying my life and family. I am very thankful to God for allowing my life to continue.

I have learned He's there even when we don't know He is or when we don't ask Him to be. I'm grateful for my story, even the horrific parts, because experience is a powerful teacher. I'm grateful for my sobriety, and I do not take it for granted. My hope is that God will continue to show me how to make a difference in the lives of others.

Do not be afraid to get sober. You can do it. I did.

HE IS FAITHFUL

KIM PRINCE

Have you ever been going along in life, thinking how good life is and that you are so blessed—only to have the rug snatched out from under you and you are left wondering, "What happened?" I have. You probably have too. But, adversity can be an opportunity for God to be glorified. My family has endured many troubles where God has shown us His love and that He walks before us and with us through all that life has for us.

In February of 2012, during worship service, I felt God tell me that our lives were going to change. But we should not worry because He was in control. I asked, "What is it, God? Is it my husband's job, cancer, the mission field?" What did that mean? Why would I choose those things? My husband's job was fine. No one in my family had ever had cancer. And at no time had we ever considered going on a mission trip.

Since I am not accustomed to hearing from God this way, I left church that day and thought, "Wow, my mind really does play tricks on me." Well, a few weeks later, it happened again. I was not sure what to do with it, so I just ignored it. But luckily, God doesn't ignore us. Over time, the feeling became so overwhelming that one day in August I shared with a friend that I wasn't sure what it meant, but I could feel, strongly, that change was coming.

A couple of weeks later, on Labor Day weekend, we were in our Sunday service and our pastor asked if anyone needed prayer. I raised my hand for a family member, and I heard a familiar voice begin to pray over my body. I wondered why he was praying for my body; it was fine. I was really wanting him to pray for my family member. Then I realized that I was distracted and resumed praying, feeling a little guilty.

The following Tuesday, September 4th, was my first pain. I remember sitting at the red light on the way to pick up my daughter from school and thinking, "I do not have time for this." But by the time we got home, I had decided to go to the medical clinic, where I was diagnosed with a urinary tract infection. They sent me home with medicine and said I would feel better the next day. Well, I didn't. I called them back, and they said to go to the Emergency Room. Since my family was at church, I drove myself and was again diagnosed with a UTI. They also said to see my regular doctor on Monday. At least they gave me some heavy pain medicine because the pain only continued to intensify. By Sunday night, I was incredibly sick. I literally did not have the strength to get out of bed. I remember telling my husband that something was really wrong with me. I was scared.

At the doctor's office the next morning at 9 a.m., my doctor came into the room and saw me sitting in the chair leaning back with my right leg extended. I could not stand any pressure on my abdomen. She looked at me and said, "You have appendicitis. You need to go to the Emergency Room." After a simple 3-minute CT scan, I was diagnosed with appendicitis and in need of "emergency" surgery. At around 8:30 that night, they finally wheeled me into surgery. After surgery, the doctor said it looked like my appendix had ruptured and then somehow repaired itself, and that it exploded when he tried to remove it.

Finally, on Friday, September 14, I was going home. As the doctor was talking to us, he said the word, carcinoma. I thought, "What? That's a cancer word." I don't remember much after hearing that word except that my husband was now sitting on my bed, holding my hand. A few minutes later, he was kneeling by my bed. I am not sure if he even realized what he was doing, but I can still remember him vividly. As the doctor left, we tried to take in what a "rare one-in-a- million appendix cancer" was doing inside of me. Shell shocked is all I can say. I was 43. I was planning my youngest daughter's Sweet 16 party.

Overwhelmed by the unknown that was before me, I came home and cried one time for just a moment and then stopped. I remembered the prayer my friend had prayed over me a couple of weeks before in church. My God had gone before me. I was distracted in that moment so that I would know that the Lord knew what was coming, and He was with me. He alone would provide the strength and confidence in Him for the coming fight. I was empowered by the Holy Spirit! It did not matter that I was fighting a cancer so rare that there were no reliable statistics for survival rates. It did not matter that this disease WAS known to reoccur in most patients. God had this! That became my motto! He had been preparing me for this moment my whole life. I could look back at the altars of remembrance in the times that I had personally witnessed God's faithfulness to my family and feel at peace that my God would be faithful to me too. It did not matter what God decided about my life, whether I lived or died. He was sovereign, and I would worship Him in this time because He is God.

After a second surgery, they only found one lymph node with cancer, so it had not spread too far. I was officially diagnosed with Stage 3 Adenocarcinoma with mucin. ***Even So***, my surgery was right on time, just like my God.

Once again it was a tough recovery. I had complications that put me in intense pain. I remember meditating on the story of Peter getting out of the boat and walking on the water toward Jesus. When Peter looked at the waves, they consumed him, but if he kept his eyes on Jesus, he could walk on water. I stayed focused on Jesus and ignored the waves around me.

In December, I started the real battle. I would get two chemotherapy doses on Tuesday and go home with a pump which infused a 3rd chemotherapy for two days. I would be asleep from Thursday until Sunday. This was our routine every other week for the next six months. After a few chemotherapy treatments, my body adjusted, and I was able to attend church on Wednesday nights, **Even So**, with my pump hissing and whirling on the 2nd row. I also was able to return to church on the Sundays right after chemotherapy. It was miraculous how God was just carrying me through this ordeal. And I will tell you, I needed to be at church. The smiles and hugs of my church family, and their encouragement, were my life line. God loved me through them.

God has never changed me so much in so little time as during my battle with cancer. I could envision a ladder reaching up to Heaven and instead of climbing one rung at time, I was jumping over three or four. He grew me above and beyond my wildest dreams. There was a joy that came from some place that I did not even know existed. The joy of the Lord, truly, was my strength. I had released the reins; I wasn't looking at the waves, and God had taken over. There was a peace that I cannot explain.

Truthfully, every day was not joyful. I had my moments. But God would not let me stay there. He counteracted every move that the Enemy would make against my joy and peace. God was always one step ahead, going before me. Every day through the next few months, I was encouraged through a card, a delivery, a visit, a phone call, or even a song on the radio. He ministered to me from every direction. I was literally covered by His mercy. I could not believe the support. I was even receiving encouragement and prayers from people I did not know. Even my sweet little nephews and niece would send up prayers for me every night. Can you imagine what that sounded like in Heaven?

Now the Enemy attacks from all directions, even through your doctors. This is the unexpected wave that comes out of nowhere. One day my allergist asked me what kind of cancer I had. I told him Stage 3 appendiceal cancer. He told me that a guy named Stuart Scott on ESPN had that and I needed to go home and look him up. Under the direction of my wise husband, I had purposely stayed away from the internet regarding my cancer. But, this sounded interesting, and I decided to read about him. He was just beginning his 3rd fight with the cancer. Although he had done well in his first two fights, he was scared and felt like he may not beat it this time. This then led me to blogs about my disease, and I became overwhelmed. I was devastated! I began to sob, and after only a couple of minutes, my doorbell rang. I did not move off of the sofa because I did not want anyone to see me in that condition. I finally went to the door and there was a package. I opened it and inside was a gift and an encouraging note from my cousins in Mississippi. I sat down on my stairs and cried and then I laughed out loud. I just looked up at heaven and wondered how I could doubt my God. He knew what I needed in that exact minute, on that exact day and had set it in motion days before I needed it. How great is our God? Sadly, Stuart Scott did pass away. However, his death did not instill in me fear. I knew cancer would not determine when I was done on this earth; God would!

I had a few more unexpected waves, including a drug re-action to one of the chemotherapies and losing my hair in the 10th treatment. *Even So*, God sustained me through it all. Let me just say that losing your hair is tough. My first outing with no hair was my daughter's school team banquet. I looked around and all of the ladies were wearing scarves and hats. Then, on my first Sunday with no hair, I walked through the church doors and realized that almost all of the ladies had on a scarf or a hat. Are you kidding me? What encouragement! God was just loving on me. He was using His children to help me walk my journey. Faithfulness!

Soon after, I told my husband that I wanted to go on the church mission trip to Bogota. I am sure this was a little out of the blue for him. I was sitting there with no hair. But he is who he is, and he was going to support me in WHATEVER!

In September of 2013, we left for Colombia! We were going to build classrooms for a school on top of the poorest mountain in Bogota. I did not have much strength and wasn't sure how much I could help on a construction trip, **Even So**, I boarded the plane. I cannot tell you how much my life was changed. I felt pretty well the first couple of days and worked fairly hard. I was contributing. But by Wednesday, I was exhausted. Needing a less intense job, I was assigned bagging the candy and school supplies which we would give to the children during Friday chapel. By Thursday, I was back on construction detail. I was picking up shovels full of cement and carrying them to my team to build brick walls for a school room for those precious children. Saturday of that week was one year, to the day, of my cancer diagnosis! The glory was all His!

That night at dinner, our pastor asked me if I would share my testimony in the service he would be preaching the next morning. Let me just say, NO! I hadn't even truly processed all that had happened to me yet. But, when God gives you a story, we have to honor Him by telling it. So, of course, I reluctantly said, "Yes." That evening as I prepared, God gave me a peace that was amazing. With the help of the Holy Spirit, my story just flowed out, even though it was my first time using an interpreter. I explained that exactly one year ago on that Saturday I was in a hospital being diagnosed with cancer, and then I had endured two surgeries and six months of chemotherapy. However, now I was standing on this mountain with them singing and worshiping the same God that my beloved church back home was worshiping. I felt the spirit of the Lord just fall upon me. HOW GREAT IS OUR GOD? Faithful!

A short time after we returned from Bogota, my pastor asked me to give my mission trip testimony to our church. In preparation, God helped me realize that on that Wednesday in Bogota, when I thought I wasn't being very useful because I was only sorting the candy and school supplies for the kids, I had physically touched every piece of candy and every pencil that every child would receive. I had been used for the kingdom of God, even in my weakness. Isn't God good?

God is still stretching me to live outside of the box that I created. 2 Timothy 2:13 (NLT) says "If we are unfaithful, he remains faithful, for he cannot deny who he is." He doesn't give up on us even in our sin and imperfect nature because He is God. He has used my experiences to help me understand that He will not give up on me—even when I am ignoring Him or disobeying Him. He will still go before me and prepare the way when change is coming. He will let me know He is there, if I choose to recognize His grace and mercy. He will help me become the woman He intended, even if I am too afraid to try. Trust me, I am a work in progress.

Another box I had chosen to dwell in was fear. Although I love to sing and worship, I was terrified to sing in front of people. My knees literally knock. During a Bible study, I learned that to not use your gifts from God is living in disobedience. I was disobeying the God that had just walked me through cancer. Well, I became undone. The Lord had put a dream in my heart, many years before, to be part of a worship team. Although I had been told that I could sing, I lived in fear of failure, and I had not made any attempts to do so. My pastor's wife could see the look on my face at the end of that night and asked what was wrong. It just fell out of my mouth. I am living in disobedience! I told her my story and she encouraged me to walk out in faith. The following week she learned that they needed another singer for the women's retreat and she suggested me. When I was asked, my first reaction was to run out of the church, but I knew that I had to do it. I knew that God was opening a door, creating an opportunity for me to trust Him and lean on Him. Within the month, I was singing at the retreat and, soon thereafter, I became a part of the worship team. I have never overcome the fear of singing in front of people, but I have learned how to lean on God completely. I did not stand on that stage alone. His presence would overwhelm me. He does not set us up to fail! I am standing on that stage by the grace of our God who put a dream in me, and I am blessed and honored to be there. If we just let go and lean on God, He will fulfill His dreams for us.

Even So, the Lord is not finished with me yet. What I have learned, through these adventures in life, is that God walks before me and He sustains me through every trial, every uncertainty. As Jeremiah says, "Because of the Lord's great love we are not consumed, for his compassions never fail. They are new every morning; great is your faithfulness" (Lamentations 3:22-23). Always remember, our suffering does not diminish God's love or faithfulness; it allows us to experience it.

FROM TRASH TO TREASURE

MARY ANN OTLEY

We have all had experiences we wish we could sweep under the carpet or make disappear. I know I have. Looking back, I have often thought, "If that experience didn't happen, my life would be different, my circumstances would be different, and 'I' would be different." For far too many years, I allowed certain circumstances to define me. The year between my eighth and ninth grade I was sexually abused. That summer the rug was swept out from underneath me and the floor beneath my feet gave way.

This happy-go-lucky kid, who enjoyed being with family, playing with my friends and babysitting for extra money, suffered traumatic and confusing experiences far beyond my understanding. Before placing a foot into high school, I was sexually abused by three different people—my dentist, a neighborhood boy, and a very close family member who

I loved and trusted. Although they were isolated incidents, I felt that they were all connected. I was convinced there was something about me that was causing me to be in the center of these horrific, terrifying, and defiling experiences. I was filled with guilt and shame.

One late night while I was clutching my pillow tight—trying to escape the unbearable feelings of shame and fear—I heard a voice speak to me, "You must be really bad for something like this to happen to you." There was only one other person who could have known what had happened to me, and I replied to who I thought was the owner of that voice. "God, I must really be bad. I am dirty and bad and disgusting." I tried to keep the words from forming, but I whispered, "I am trash." And although, some trash is restorable, the trash I identified with was unsalvageable, closer to a used piece of tissue someone blew their nose in and threw away. I was damaged goods of the worst kind. The challenge was—how to hide that from the rest of the world.

The weight of my new identity was crushing. I began having recurring nightmares where I was guided down a long dark hallway to a door. When I entered the room, before me there was a beautiful circle of light. It was alive, vibrant, brilliant. I could feel its brilliance in the depths of who I was. I believe this light was my soul.

My heart sank when a drop of darkness fell from an unseen ceiling. I saw the slow drip and could not stop it before it fell with its obscure gloom and despair and invaded the peace and purity of the brilliant light. Then another drop fell, and another and another until my soul was no longer white, but it was covered in darkness. There was only a speck of light that tried its best to shine through. As I focused hopelessly on the little light that courageously shined through the darkness, I recognized a voice from the night—I clutched my pillow, "You have one more chance." I woke up with my heart racing, feeling the shame in my dark and tainted soul. I asked God to forgive me for being so bad and told Him, "I'll do better, somehow, I'll figure out how."

My parents' divorce forced us into poverty. After graduating from high school, I enrolled in a certificate program to be trained as an executive assistant. Naively, my goal was to move to Chicago, be discovered, become rich and famous, and have the resources to take care of my mom and siblings. *How? I'll figure that out when I get there.*

Chicago is a beautiful city, full of opportunities and full of snares. It wasn't long before I was on my own, just scraping by and dealing with the harsh realities of life. I met a new group of friends from work and joined them for a dinner in Greek Town one Friday night after work. After dinner, I placed my money on the table to pay for dinner and visited the ladies' room. When I returned to the table, my new friends were gone. They had forgotten me. We didn't have cell phones then, and I didn't have money for a cab ride all the way back to the suburbs. Hours passed, and the truth set in that I needed a way to get home. A guy coming from the bar approached me, shared he had noticed I had been waiting at the door for a long time and asked if he could help me. I explained my circumstances, and he said he would be happy to help. I felt rescued as I entered into his black sports car. "We have to make a quick stop on the way to drop off something to a friend," he told me as we drove up to a massive apartment complex. "You should come with me, so you are not sitting here alone."

I followed him in, up the elevator, down a hall, and into the apartment. The apartment was dark. There was no friend. He took advantage of my naivete and I was raped. Panic stricken and fearing for my life, I was paralyzed. *Will I make it out alive?* That was the thought I asked in my head. Thank God, this guy stayed true to his promise and drove me home. We drove in silence as I directed him to my new friend's apartment building. I did not want him to know where I lived or what my car looked like. After he drove away, I ran to my car, drove home, and tried to wash the guilt, shame and sickening scent of cologne off of me. It was humiliating. *How naïve could I be? Now what do I do?*

The old feelings of shame, fear and trashiness that I had managed to push down when arriving in Chicago—they all reappeared. Heaps of condemnation poured upon me continually.

It wasn't long before I was dating the wrong guys, drinking myself to sleep, smoking two packs of Marlboro Lights a day, and snorting cocaine on the weekends—to escape the pain. I just didn't understand how life works. I vowed to find my way and I began searching for answers. I lived according to *Cosmopolitan* and *Glamor*. I memorized lyrics of the popular songs to find meaning. I went to movies and studied characters to learn who to be. I devoured *People* magazine to learn from celebrities how to live. I watched Oprah religiously to get the next best advice on relationships. What I didn't know is that all these resources are not exactly designed to equip us and help us, but rather to keep us hooked to buy the next month's issue, go to the next movie, and watch tomorrow's Oprah show. Answers were always just around the corner. So, I started reading self-help books, meditated on positive affirmations, and researched different religions and beliefs. I read that knowledge is power, so I tried to consume knowledge, about everything. However, year after year, it still felt like I was a pinball in a pinball machine, bouncing from crisis to crisis.

I made a decision that I believed would make everything better. I got married. Long story short, I was three hours from home when my car broke, and I was bombarded with expletives and a man screaming through the phone that now we would have to use our money to pay for my @$*! car, instead of buying a fishing boat for him. Click.

That was the game changer. At 32 years old, I had never felt more alone and abandoned. I stood in the gas station—somewhere in the middle of Indiana—crushed and full of questions. *I just don't get it. What's real? What's important? What's the truth?* These same three questions were repeated over and over in my mind. *What's real? What's important? What's the truth?*

"You got AAA?" came a question from behind the counter. "Yes. My father-in-law gave it to us for a Christmas present."

"Smart man. Great present. You're going to need it."

An hour later I was in the front seat of a tow truck, being driven from somewhere in Indiana to St. Louis. When I got home, I poured a glass of wine, sat on my deck that overlooked a little lake, and found myself screaming to the stars at the top of my lungs, "What's real?!" "What's important?!" "What's the truth?!"

I was at my wit's end. I didn't expect an answer from the night sky, but I got one. From the depths of my being a prayer bubbled up and out of my mouth. I met each verse with skepticism.

Our Father (*You aren't real, are You?*)
Who art in Heaven, (It's *not a real place, right?*)
Hallowed be Thy Name, (*What does "hallowed" mean anyway?*)
Thy Kingdom come, (Is that like a *fairy tale?*)

Thy will be done here on earth as it is in heaven,
  (*Does that mean I can still buy the clothes I like?*)
Give us this day our daily bread. (*What about a car,
  a house, or success?*)
Forgive us our sins, (*Can't happen.*)
As we forgive those who sin against us (*Won't happen.*)
Lead us not into temptation, (*Why would You do that?*)
Deliver us from evil . . . (*No one is big enough to
  do that.*)

As skeptical as I was about the prayer, I couldn't stop praying it. My marriage lasted no more than six months and I started a new career. I knew something had happened that night when I cried to the stars. I had a renewed sense of hope, and I continued to pray that prayer.

The people I worked with now were different from any other workplace. They were kind and considerate. They worked with purpose and passion. I became attracted to one person, in particular, and I felt he was attracted to me too. Tom and I met for dinner one evening when he asked me about my thoughts on God. I was disappointed. I didn't want a Jesus freak of a guy. I looked him square in the eye and told him, "Listen, when I was a little girl, I bought this stuff. I 'tried' Jesus. I found the truth. Jesus doesn't work."

He looked right back at me and without batting an eye he replied, "What, Mary Ann? *Love* doesn't work for you?" I was surprised by his confidence and composure. I thought for sure I had closed the conversation. "What does *love* have to do with *Jesus?*" I asked. He leaned in, looked at me with conviction, and said, "You can search the world and research every religion, but you will never find a God that left His throne, came to the earth, was rejected, beaten, spit on and mocked, nailed to a tree to die, just to redeem those very people to Himself. Jesus has everything to do with love."

Something happened inside of me, Tom continued, "Mary Ann, I don't know who hurt you, but it wasn't Jesus. If you run from Him, you are running from your only hope of healing." *How did he know I had been hurt?* Tears stung my eyes. "Then why did he allow such terrible things to happen to me?" I asked sincerely. "I don't know what happened to you, but I know this, Jesus didn't do those things to you. Lost, broken, wounded people hurt you, not Jesus," Tom said gently. I had always thought that I caused terrible things to happen to me. This was the first time anyone ever gave me an explanation about what happened to me that made sense. Lost, broken and wounded people hurt me. "You think Jesus can help me?" I asked Tom. "I know He can. He has been waiting for you to ask?" I fell in love with Tom, and I fell in love with Jesus.

Jesus answered the cries of my heart when I hit bottom, but I had no idea how faithful He would be to answer my cries now. Tom and I married, and we had three beautiful children. I wrestled with Jesus often and found that when I was transparent with Him, He always revealed Himself to me in ways that helped me understand or take the next step I needed in my life. But, in my forties, I became very ill. I slept 20 hours a day while our church family took care of our children and they brought a warm dinner to our family each night. It was humiliating. I loved my children, and I wanted to be part of their daily lives. I begged God for help and wall-papered my kitchen with every promise He highlighted to me during my daily Bible reading times.

Then God brought Elsie into my life. Elsie was an inter-cessor in her late seventies who compassionately took me to Jesus in a way I had never experienced Him.

Tom and I attended a conference that explained that God's design for each family is that the father leads by bless-ing his family. The father's blessing includes leading in hu-mility and truth, serving in love, imparting God-given iden-tity to each family member, and preparing each child for their future.

We broke into groups to pray, and Elsie was the prayer leader. As we prayed, I was feeling grief for the loss of God's design for a family in my life, tears began to flow from my eyes. I couldn't stop them. Elsie sat in front of me and asked me if God was revealing something to me. I nodded tearfully, "I can't go there Elsie. It's too painful." The counselors and psychologists that I sought out in my past all wanted me to go back to this night from my childhood, but when I did, it only made things worse. "I can't do it."

Elsie placed my hands into hers and looked me in the eyes, "Mary Ann, let's let Jesus do the work this time."

I stared into her eyes. Love and confidence stared back.

"Ok," I whispered. "Mary Ann, what are you feeling right now?" Elsie asked gently.

"I am afraid. I am terrified really," I answered.

"Anything else?"

"I am alone. I don't know what is going to happen to me. I don't know who is going to take care of me." The words came unexpectedly through my heavy sobs.

"What else are you feeling, sweetheart?" Elsie asked.

"I am so disappointed and discouraged. And I am afraid I am a disappointment."

"Anything else?" Elsie asked.

"No."

Elsie then held my hands and prayed with me and told Jesus everything I told her. For the first time in my life, I felt like someone truly listened to me and as she shared my emotions with Jesus, hope sprung up in my heart. Then she asked me, "What did Jesus reveal to you that caused these emotions to come forth so strongly?" I was feeling grief for the loss of God's design for a family in my life, cautiously I answered, "I was abused when I was young by several people, but there was one person that wounded me the most. The vision that came to me during this prayer time was the night when my dad came into my room," I shared.

Elsie was not moved. She was as steady as a rock, and simply asked, "Jesus, what do You want Mary Ann to know about that night?"

With my eyes closed, I saw Jesus was in the room. He was radiant, beautiful, strong and kind. I had never felt so safe. We weren't alone, though. Someone else was in the room. I turned my head to look toward Dad, and a 9-foot demon towered over Dad. I gasped, "Elsie there is a demon towering over Dad!" I recognized how it made me feel. And instantly I realized that this evil creature has been tormenting me all my life."

Elsie was not shocked, and she simply asked, "Lord, what do you want to do with that 9-foot demon?" I closed my eyes and was back in the room where I witnessed Jesus take a push pin, poke the Demon in the center of its being and pin it to the wall. Jesus looked at me and said, "He will never torment you again."

My whole body sighed with relief. I looked at Dad—no longer with fear, but with compassion. I told Elsie what I saw Jesus do and she asked, "Can you forgive your Dad?" I looked at how much Jesus loved Dad. I knew in an instant that I had not been battling flesh and blood all my life, but principalities, powers and spiritual hosts of wickedness in high places. They play on people's vulnerabilities and insecurities and influence us by robbing us of our dignity, tormenting us and lying to us about our identity. I wondered what had happened to Dad that brought him to this place. What he did was wrong, but he could be redeemed—not by modern psychology or drugs, but by Jesus. I said, "Yes. I forgive Him. What he did was wrong, but I want him to be well."

I had always heard that pedophiles can never be helped. But when I saw the power Jesus had over that dark intruder, I knew there was hope. I just had to put my hope in the right place and the right person.

Then Elsie asked, "Jesus, who is Mary Ann to You? I was afraid of His answer because I knew who I was. Deep down I was bad, dirty, and disgusting trash. I couldn't look at Him, but He stood in front of me with a brilliant white gown in His hands. It resembled the beautiful soul I had seen in my dreams, years and years before. He placed it over my head like a father would place a dress on his little girl. It felt light and I felt holy. Then He placed a simple gold crown upon my head, a ring on my finger and sandals on my feet. He looked at me with love that cannot be expressed with words and said to me, "You are my princess." I had never felt so prized, accepted and loved in my life. I didn't know that love like this was possible. I fell into Him and cried while the lies were being washed away by the love that God lavished upon me. My identity was established. I was Jesus' princess.

I found the answers to my heartfelt questions.

What is real? Jesus is real, and so is His enemy. There are two kingdoms that are warring over our minds, our thoughts, our strength, our identity, our being.

What is important? You are. And I am. People are important to God.

What is the truth? Jesus is the truth. He holds the truth about who we are, what we need and how we live. His truth sets us free. There isn't anyone or anything He can't heal, restore and redeem.

If you have suffered abuse of any kind, and if you are carrying intense feelings of fear, guilt or shame, I encourage you to never stop seeking and beholding Jesus. He alone holds the keys to your healing and freedom. Those powerful keys are His infinite love. Call to Jesus, He will answer you and make you His.

MOVING FROM MY COMFORT ZONE

ROULA KAHLIL

As I commenced my journey from my homeland of "Lebanon" to the US, suddenly I felt completely alone—even though I was surrounded by lots of people. As I sat in my seat, looking at the clouds through the tiny window, I found myself uncertain about the decision I had made. I asked the Lord, "Is it the right decision that I made? Have I lost my mind to leave all that is familiar and all of my loved ones to move to a new foreign land?" It scared me to death when I started to think of all the "unknowns" that were about to unfold. I know that I heard the Lord's voice saying, "YES!" I was being obedient to His voice and putting my trust in Him, but now doubts were flooding my thoughts. The trip was so long—it felt like it would never end. Everyone that I knew dreamed of living in the greatest country on earth— the USA—to live the American dream. But my journey was not for that earthly dream, but indeed, for the eternal dream.

I was born and raised in Lebanon, a beautiful country positioned in the heart of the Middle East. But evil has destroyed it. While I was growing up, war after war broke out. I witnessed gun shootings, missiles launching, explosions everywhere, and aircrafts striking. These sounds of war were the only lullabies that I heard in my childhood and teenage years.

Did I regret it? Yes! I hated seeing people getting killed and witnessing the violence and the evil acts. No child should have to live through the hatred and divisions that occurred—even among family members—for their political convictions.

But I do not regret my journey because it shaped me to become who I am today. Yes, I have decided to follow Jesus in the midst of all this chaos because He is the Prince of Peace. When there is no peace on earth, there is peace with Christ and in Him alone!

Living in your comfort zone is the best thing until you recognize the damage you do to yourself by not allowing God to take you out of this comfort zone—to where He desires to place you. He will take you for a great journey full of adventure. It's all about walking with Him by faith.

The pilot announced that we were approaching the Atlanta airport and would soon land. My heart was super excited to see my husband and start my life as a newly married woman. The plane landed safely, and all the passengers started getting off the plane. My first impression was, "Oh my, is this just an airport?" The airport was huge—I mean gigantic! I had never seen such a big airport—super neat and so organized. There was even a train to take passengers from the terminal to the baggage claim. To be honest, I was scared to get on the train because I thought I'd find myself somewhere in the city and I would be lost. That was the start of my life in a huge and unique city in the USA.

I often hear people say that they would like to live in the "land of opportunities," the "land of freedom," but I have never felt the desire to move away from Lebanon or to not serve the Lord in my homeland. I was comfortable being in the warmth of my family, friends, and church. But obviously God had a different plan for me, so here I am—starting a new adventure.

The United States is a huge country. It's like you are looking into a magnifying glass. So now begins my journey of learning everything about how to live in the United States. I entered as a child enters this world, and I started grasping and learning everything I could, so I would fit into this new world. That was me now. Shopping trips are like going through an obstacle course, shopping for things I have never heard of, and there are so many options—it's hard to know what to choose. Everything is different in the USA (food, clothing, driving, laws, and people). I love having a house and a big yard—all for my husband and me—but it comes with quietness. Quietness is something I had never experienced since I came from a large, busy city.

In the Middle Eastern culture, you expect visitors at any moment, but my regular visitors now are the robins, cardinals, hummingbirds, and squirrels. My adventure started by learning how to accept quietness in my new life. Furthermore, my husband was involved in a ministry that required him to travel for a full month at a time. That was an extreme experience of quietness, in addition to feeling alone on this huge continent. In those early days I spent a big amount of time crying, missing my folks and Lebanon. It was hard for the youngest in a big family to move away from everyone else. Remembering the sadness of my dad and the distress of my mom—seeing their daughter leave them—was tough. Still today, this memory brings tears to my eyes. ***Even So***, God knew about my feelings and He was preparing me to accept this state of quietness. As I met a new godly friend, I learned why the Lord put me in such a situation of "quietness."

There is another word for quietness—a solitary place. Aha, do you recall Jesus' words in the Bible: "*Very early in the morning, while it was still dark, Jesus got up, left the house and went off to a solitary place, where he prayed (Mark 1:35). My friend understood the life of an immigrant, especially the situation I was in*—no family, no friends and even my husband was away. She started telling me about that verse and the importance of spending time in a solitary place—to be in the presence of the Almighty. You might say, "But you are Christian, and this is method 101 in a Christian life." Yes, you are right, but believe me, knowing it in your head is different than applying it in your personal life with the full depth that His Word brings. God's plan started to be revealed to me, little by little. Being in God's presence was my runaway place because it was a place of comfort and peace. Going back to Lebanon to visit was my complete desire, but I had to trust in His provision of a plane ticket and the right timing to go back to see my family. I had to live with a positive attitude and a spirit of contentment—knowing that He had never let me down.

My husband and I shared one car since our finances didn't allow us to buy another car. One day, while he was on a trip, I decided to surprise him by getting my driver's license. I had searched and started the process of studying the driving rules and the street signs to apply for my license. And here I was before the test—excited and proud of myself for being independent and trying to start putting my feet on the ground. I was tired of being dependent on others for everything I did or needed. Success! When my husband walked in the door from his trip, I was holding my driver's license in my hand! Surely the Lord has helped me!

My husband has made many quality friends in the States, and everyone was waiting to meet the woman who stole his heart. We have had so many fellowships with American friends that welcomed me. I was so terrified of making any cultural mistakes, so I started observing how people talked, acted, dressed and how they ate. But I soon discovered that my observations were not enough. One day I thought I was being friendly with a couple who was my husband's friends. I asked the lady about her due date and if she knew the gender of the baby. Oh my! That was the biggest mistake I had ever done. The couple was so offended, and they spoke with my husband to help educate me. The lady was not pregnant—she just had a belly. To be honest, I was shocked by their reaction—even though I was wrong with my assumption. I learned my lesson the hard way. Since then I have learned to mind my own business and be super careful about the subject of my conversations. Slowly but surely, I have learned how to live the American life and understand the culture.

Since I was little, church on Sunday was not to be missed. My husband and I joined a church that was good in size for America—but not for me. The church had about 3000 members and we had built so many friendships there, but it was huge. People were in every corner of the church (lobby, sanctuary, Sunday school classes and even the balcony). It was so big in my eyes and even though I spoke English, I needed translation to understand the preacher because it seemed like he could speak all the Bible in 30 minutes. The biggest church in Lebanon holds a maximum of 500 people, but the church I came from had 200 members. We all knew one another by name. If someone missed a worship service, we all would be asking about them and even visiting them to make sure they were fine. We had friends in this church, but we could count them on our fingers.

Later, the Lord has blessed us with two beautiful daughters. They are the light of my life. Going through the pregnancy experience for the first time and in a foreign country was a school by itself. I have learned so many things about how well they care for the baby and mother. I have also noticed how demanding it is to have everything ready for a child (room, stroller, car seat, etc.). The hardest thing is when I was asked to start a baby registry at some store. I had no idea about a baby's requirements first of all and secondly, usually people in my country of Lebanon brought you a gift of their choice after the baby was born. They would come to visit the family and to meet the new born child. Learning about the baby registry and having a baby shower was all new to me. To be honest, I have enjoyed the system better than what we did in Lebanon, and I was excited to learn the new American way. As our oldest was going to preschool, my world opened up to new learning opportunities for me—the systems and procedures, the teacher's conferences and celebrating the little ones' events. It was all fun and I promise that I still am learning as she moves up grade by grade. Curriculum, school clubs, and problem solving are all on a different level for me as it is a different generation, and I am from different culture. As much as I have adopted my new culture, there is a big part of me that still screams my Middle Eastern culture. My heart has never left my country and the Middle Eastern people.

After many years of being in the States and asking the Lord what He wants from me here—what is my purpose—what is His will? I think the Lord has shown up and revealed His plan for me. My husband who has been involved in International Ministries has heard the Lord's voice clearly to leave everything and start our own ministry, serving our people—the persecuted ones in the Middle East and He has promised to be with us. We have now spent many nights and days in prayer, knowing that stepping into the unknown as a family is not an easy task. But He has promised never to let His people down. God prepared the path for me to this moment. Now, I serve the Lord and the people that I love from the States in ways that I would have never been able to accomplish being in Lebanon.

Maybe the Lord delays to show us His plan for our life but being in His will and waiting patiently is the key for being prepared and ready for the task when it is revealed.

This is the promise that never left me and was my source of encouragement every time I felt down. "Have I not commanded you? Be strong and courageous. Do not be afraid; do not be discouraged, for the LORD your God will be with you wherever you go" (Joshua 1:9).

MY JOURNAL TO HOLLAND

ROXANNE SAFFLES

PART 1

Journal entry
February 3, 1998

"I have told you all this so that you may have peace in me. Here on earth you will have many trials and sorrows. But take heart, because I have overcome the world" (John 16:33).

God, thank You for literally forcing me go on the College and Career ski trip. The skiing was great, but the fellowship is what I needed so badly.

Some days are such a struggle that it's not even a day-by-day process, but moment-by-moment. I am still so heart broken andcan't imagine how I could ever feel like a whole person again.

Nevertheless, You provided the way for me to go and you helped me to be still, to look around, to take in the beauty of the majestic snow-covered mountains, and to be thankful and grateful for what I do have.

I know you are still in control and will take care of me and the kids.

October 3, 1997 was the day that changed my life forever. It was the day of my husband's very sudden, devastating death. Brian Tribble was the music minister at Centercrest Baptist Church in the Birmingham, Alabama, area. He was at the church in the early morning hours getting ready for a men's trip to Washington, D.C., when he was shot and killed by a burglar—stealing less than $20 from a coke machine in the Church building. I was twenty-eight years old with four small children—ages six months, two, three, and seven years old. I started dating Brian when I was sixteen, and we had just had our tenth wedding anniversary. He was all I knew and I could not imagine how I would ever feel whole again, much less be able to open my heart to love again the way I loved him. ***Even So***, after a short period of time and as much as I did not want this to be my lot in life, I knew I couldn't have Brian back. I told God on many occasions, "I don't like this, and I don't understand this, BUT I choose to trust and love You anyway." You see, God had shown me through many other life experiences, both good and bad, that He was in control of my life and that regardless of how I felt, He would remain faithful, and He would heal my broken heart. God showed me daily, through people, cards, messages, billboards, His Word, and even a candy heart on my Valentine's Day cupcake that said, "Trust Me." He would remain faithful and was going to make me whole again. He would heal my wounds so that my "scars" were barely even visible, as only He, the Master Physician, could do.

I truly do not understand how those without faith make it through this kind of tragedy. I Thessalonians 4:13 says, "And now, dear brothers and sisters, we want you to know what will happen to the believers who have died so that you will not grieve like people who have no hope." As a follower of Christ, I knew Brian was in a much better place—a perfect place—but I grieved for what my kids and I were missing by him not being here to share this life with us. Nothing was "normal" or "right" without Brian, but God is the ultimate healer. Through God's grace and guidance, He was healing our hearts as we were creating a "new normal."

December 3, 1998

"The Lord will guide you always. He will satisfy your needs" (Isaiah 58:11).

God, I don't know if I'm ready to start dating again, but I know I don't want to be by myself for

the rest of my life. I know You are all I need —
I know you are enough—but I need skin (lol). Also,
I really don't want to kiss a bunch of toads, so could
you please just send me the prince.

I prayed this prayer exactly two months after the one-year anniversary of Brian's death. One year is not the magic number, but I had at least faced every milestone, both big and small, once—so if I'd done it once I could do it again, right? That must have been what every person in my life was thinking because it felt like everybody I knew was trying to set me up with somebody. I felt like the only realist, thinking, "Who in the world is going to want a 29-year-old woman with four small children?" Besides that, Brian was all I knew, so how would I ever make it work with someone else? Could I love someone else the way I loved Brian? Was I just looking for a replacement or a true partner and friend? Then I came across this poem by an unknown author— "A Trip to Italy."

Planning our lives is like planning a fabulous
vacation to Italy. You learn all you can about Ita-
ly—you read guide books and even learn the lan-
guage. You get on the airplane ready to enjoy your
trip to Italy. As you are about to land, a cheery flight
attendant says, "Welcome to Holland." What do

you mean Holland? I'm going to Italy! All my life I've dreamed of going to Italy. The flight attendant explains that there has been a change in plans— Holland is where you have landed, and Holland is where you will stay. Although devastated at first, after the shock of it all, you go out and buy a new guide book to learn a whole new language and way of life, and you meet a whole new group of people you never would have met. Eventually you begin to realize that they haven't taken you to a disgusting place full of pestilence, famine and disease—it's just a different place. It's slower paced than Italy, less flashy than Italy, but after you've been there a while and catch your breath, you discover that Holland has windmills, Holland has tulips, Holland even has Rembrandts. But everyone you know is busy coming and going from Italy and bragging about their wonderful time in Italy. For the rest of your life you will say, "Yes, that's where I was supposed to go, that's what I had planned." And the pain of that experience will never completely go away—because the loss of a dream is a very significant loss. But if you spend your entire life mourning the fact that you didn't get to Italy, you may never be free to enjoy the special and very lovely things about Holland!

Losing Brian was not how I had envisioned my life, but I believe in a God of restoration. Although this might not have been my original destination and at times it was a place I did NOT want to be, as I lived one day at a time, God was creating my Holland. Ultimately, there would even come a day when I could not imagine being anywhere but Holland.

Brian and I had a wonderful marriage, but I knew when I decided to take that step and begin dating again, I had to focus on my present and future relationships— and not compare the two. One would not be better than the other—they would just be different.

December 25, 1998

"Now all glory to God, who is able, through his mighty power at work within us, to accomplish infinitely more than we might ask or think"
(Ephesians 3:20).

I went on my first date Wednesday night, December 23, with Tommy Saffles. I had a really nice time. He even called yesterday. I was kind of expecting him to call today, but he didn't. I realized that I was looking for a phone call to make me happy and I was not turning to the real source of happiness— You, GOD. You are so sufficient and you're teaching me to be content, and to just be still and be with

You—especially on this Christmas Day. Today was still hard, but I didn't have to just endure—You helped me through it with a greater appreciation of Your love for me! This is the day that You, oh Lord, have made.

Every day after this, Tommy and I either spoke on the phone or saw each other. This marked the beginning of a new chapter in our lives. God had brought this wise, Godly, not to mention good-looking, man into my life like a whirlwind as he jumped in with both feet. He had sent my prince. Tommy had been divorced for eight years when we met, and he had struggled with whether to even call me that first time. Who could blame him? A woman with four children (three of whom were under 4-years-old) was quite an undertaking. Despite his hesitation, he felt God's hand at work and chose to trust in this calling. Within two months we were engaged, and within six months we were married.

We married on June 5, 1999 and soon after moved into the home we built together with our six children—his two girls, my three girls, and my son. Staci had just graduated from high school and Dana was a Senior in high school. Katelyn, McKinley, Jake Scott, and Bailey were nine, four, three, and two. From the very beginning we taught them that although they were not born into the same family, God had brought our families together. To this day, they do not use the term "step" brother or sister. In the first years of our marriage, one or two of them tried to use the "he's not my dad" card—in which I quickly put a stop to by explaining to them that although he may not be their biological father, God had placed him in this position as their dad, so regardless of what they chose to call him, he was their Dad, and they were to treat him with the respect of one. The three youngest have always called him "Dad," but it came a little harder for Katelyn. Since she was nine and remembered Brian, she felt like it was betraying him to call someone else "Dad." We did not push the issue or force anything on any of them, and although she never felt comfortable calling him "Dad," she considers him her dad and introduces us as her Mom and Dad. Now don't get me wrong, I still feel like God had sent me my Prince, but our life was no fairytale. It was a learning process—all over again. Some of the issues that I thought I had "mastered" the first time were the very ones that I struggled with, so God was continually working on them with me. God definitely has His ways of keeping us humble. Any time two people are brought together, much less eight, there will be differences, not only in opinions, but also in the daily routine of things. But, when we keep our priority and focus on God, He is faithful to work it out in a way that leaves no doubt that it is Him at work.

PART 2

Through lots of prayers, tears, laughter, and by the grace of God, all six of our children have grown up to be great individuals who love Jesus and serve in various capacities in their churches and communities. Raising children is hard and throughout the teenage years, I was not positive we would all survive. As Proverbs 22:6 says, "Train up a child in the ways he should go and when he is old, he will not depart from it." Tommy and I had discussed how we would parent before we ever married, and we both agreed on a proactive approach rather than reactive. However, our disciplining tactics were very different. We had many conversations and compromises throughout the years, but the key to successfully molding our children into unique, Godly, independent adults was count-less numbers of prayers—along with communication, com-mitment, and consistency on our parts.

Communication was the factor that Tommy and I strug-gled with the most. We each came from homes growing up that had completely different parenting styles. We had also both been married before, and whether right or wrong, you get accustomed to doing things a certain way and you bring that with you into new relationships. Sometimes this was so difficult for us that we would not communicate at all—but I definitely do not recommend that method for anyone. How-ever, through the years and with God's help, we have learned how to better communicate with one another.

Children thrive in environments where they feel safe and secure, physically and emotionally. I have always felt like it was all right for our children to see us disagree and even have arguments, as long as they also saw remorse and forgiveness at the end of it. Children need to see that although life is hard and definitely not perfect, they can work through it and come out on the other side—even stronger than before. To be honest, there were times when Tommy and I both felt like quitting, but we did not. God has honored our obedience of commitment to each other, and He has blessed us with this amazing family. On top of that, we are leaving a legacy of commitment, modeled by a long and happy marriage for our children and grandchildren.

We also felt like it was important for our kids to know that we were committed to them as well. Even though it was difficult to get them each to all the places they needed to be—practice, games, lessons, church, etc., we wanted them to be involved in individual and team activities that would instill in them a work ethic and build their character. When you have that many children, you cannot physically be at everything. But, we were at as many as we could possibly be. Sometimes we would divide and conquer—where we would each go in a different direction. And at other times we would miss several events in order to go to one of them together—just to be able to see each other. Each one of the children knew we tried our best to be there for them, but there were times we missed some pretty special events in their lives. We taught them that although we could not always be there, God was always there for them. People will let us down even when they do not intend to, but God will never let us down. Psalms 39:7 states, *"And so Lord, where do I put my hope? My only hope is in you."*

Last, but certainly not least, is maintaining consistency. When the kids knew that Tommy and I were working together to instruct and discipline them, they were less likely to argue our rules and guidelines, or worse, to rebel against them. We were the 'mean' parents who made our children wait until they were fifteen years old to get a cell phone—and sometimes this seemed like more of a punishment for Tommy and me. It would have been so much easier to allow them to get a phone sooner, but easiest is not always the best. Technology can be useful and helpful, but it can also be destructive when used inappropriately. We just wanted our children to be old enough to make wise decisions on how to effectively use their technology and not abuse it. In this world of instant everything, we also wanted to give them something to look forward to and have to wait on. We were also consistent with our household rules and the consequences for breaking them. They did not have televisions, nor could they take their phones into their bedrooms. Also, each one had age appropriate daily chores and responsibilities to complete. Although they hated these rules when they were growing up, they are all appreciative as adults that we cared enough to stick to our convictions.

One year after the two older girls were already married, we took the four younger ones on a vacation. We went zip lining and white-water rafting on the Nantahala River. At the beginning of the trip, we took up each of their phones and put them away for the remainder of the trip. After the shock wore off and they stopped pouting, they had the best time together and with us. As we were headed home, all four of them thanked us for taking their phones and said that this had been their favorite vacation ever. I realize our situation is different than many blended families in that my four children did not have another parent to run to or to play us against each other. But I feel that as long as we showed them a common front and remained consistent, even when one of us did not completely agree, our kids knew they were not going to get away with much and in the long run respected us for it.

We haven't always had "great times" while raising all of these children. We have had some bad times in our marriage, as well. We have each felt discontentment and disillusionment at times in the direction our marriage was headed. We have struggled in the parenting department, wondering if we were doing the right things and just hoping and praying that we were effectively molding our children into Godly adults—especially when some days they did not even like us a little bit. But God has been so faithful, and He wastes nothing. He has instead used it to draw Tommy and me together to form an even stronger bond and have an even stronger love for each other. He has shown us how faithful He truly is by blessing us with an extremely close family, with children who love each other unconditionally with their whole hearts and are there for each other through the good and bad times in life. We also now have nine grandchildren to love on and spoil, but most importantly to show them the love of our Lord and Savior, Jesus Christ. I am extremely thankful and grateful that God sent Tommy Saffles into my life and that he decided to take the leap to invest not only in my life, but my children's lives as well.

In today's society, the word "family" has broadened to include all sorts of situations and some variety of a "blended family" probably makes up the majority of these. Although every family has its own qualities, characteristics and quirks, it is only by the grace of God that we do not have to just endure our situations, but we can thrive and excel in them. This can only happen when we allow God to be the common thread that holds our lives together. Because "humanly" speaking, it is impossible. *Even So*, ". . . with God, everything is possible" (Matthew 19:26).

BEAUTY FROM ASHES

SARA COLQUHOUN

I placed the test on the counter and held my breath. Not three minutes later I knew my life had changed forever. There were two pink lines. I was pregnant.

When I was seventeen years old I heard the diagnosis Polycystic Ovarian Syndrome for the first time. I was no stranger to painful cycles, irregular periods, and the all too familiar trouble with losing weight after having no problems gaining it. I didn't necessarily think anything was wrong, but wanted to hear that from a doctor. After running blood work and doing an ultrasound, it was confirmed, and within an instant, I became <u>one out of ten</u>. To this day, there is still no cure for PCOS, only ways to help manage the symptoms.

I had always envisioned being a mom, and when the diagnosis came I held back my tears. You see, one of the major side effects of having PCOS is infertility, along with the likelihood of miscarriage, which can be upwards of 45-50%. I was shocked.

Being a senior in high school at the time of diagnosis, I had no prospects of a future spouse, but knew that one day we would have to have a hard, in-depth conversation about what the future looked like in regards to having children. I left the appointment that day feeling a bit deflated, but seeing as though I wasn't actively trying to have a baby, and was just shy of eighteen, I did my best to push my feelings aside.

When my husband and I met a couple years later, during a five-month mission trip to East Africa, one of the first things that bonded us was our mutual love for children. We both excitedly expressed how we wanted to have a houseful one day of our own, as well as become Foster-to-adopt parents. I had never met a guy that felt the same way I did in regards to having so many kids, so I knew I needed to keep my eye on him. As our relationship progressed, not two years later, we found ourselves walking down the aisle.

It was during our season of engagement when I brought the topic of kids back up. I explained to Jeremy, my husband-to-be, what my diagnosis was, and what the doctors had said a few years earlier. After much prayer and thought, we decided, once married, we would start trying to conceive right away since it was likely to take some time.

The first few months flew by, and we didn't pay much attention to my reoccurring cycle. After six months, a handful of meltdowns, and a combination of what I'm sure was at least a couple dozen pregnancy tests, we felt like the next step was to consult a doctor.

We scheduled a doctor's appointment in the middle of February, roughly seven months into trying. I didn't want to get my hopes up, but my cycle had been late that month, and I wrestled with taking a pregnancy test before going to the doctor, or just having them do one there in the office. Just a little back history on yours truly, I'm traditionally not a very patient person. So, it came as a shock to no one, when one day during my lunch break, I walked across the street and bought a test. This time, I didn't tell Jeremy I was taking it. The unspoken sadness, paired with what I assumed was disappointment, became almost too much to handle. I figured, hey, if it was negative, I didn't have to tell him.

I opened the package, followed the instructions and placed the test on the counter.

I waited three minutes and gasped. I had never gotten a positive pregnancy test, only negative, so when I saw two faint pink lines I didn't know if it was a fluke or not. I took a picture and sent it to my sister. The iPhone dots seemed to be moving in slow motion before a response appeared. She saw what I saw, it was positive.

I couldn't believe it. I felt excited, scared, nervous, nauseous, and wanted to tell Jeremy immediately. After getting two positive tests, I wanted to get one more with a digital reader so I could show him as soon as he walked in the door from work that day. I stopped at another store on my way home, and through some fluke of its own, it read negative. My mind raced. How was that possible? Was it just too late in the day? Had I drunk too much water? The questions were endless, but as I waited for Jeremy to get home that day, all I felt was empty.

Jeremy met me that night, I was a crying mess. I explained what had transpired during the day, and why I couldn't stop the tears. My sweet husband, being the voice of reason, suggested we eat something and get a good night's rest. We would take the final test in the morning.

I fell asleep praying that night, that God would show up and would let a miracle happen. I wanted to believe it. I wanted to believe my spoken prayers were reaching the Almighty, but if I'm honest, I'm not sure I wholeheartedly believed it. My faith up until this point in my life had been pretty easy. I had struggled with a few things in my past, but not to the depths of having to really trust and rely on Jesus with something this big. Having a positive test and then living with the fear of losing the baby, to me, felt worse than not being able to get pregnant at all. I lived in this dark space and had a hard time seeing the light.

After not sleeping a wink, I crept out of bed around 5 a.m. to take the final test. When the timer finished blinking, it was confirmed: I was pregnant.

I gently crawled back into bed and kissed my sleeping husband on the cheek. He slowly awoke, and I whispered in his ear "we're having a baby."

We laid there that morning speaking in hushed tones of names, and where we were going to move once we had the baby, as our one-bedroom apartment wasn't big enough for our growing family. I counted the weeks and proudly exclaimed we'd have an October baby. As our alarms went off a few minutes later, I was still in awe of our new reality.

I called the doctor at 8:01 a.m. exactly that morning and scheduled our first ultrasound.

The next two weeks felt like an eternity. Jeremy and I decided that we were going to tell our immediate families that we were expecting, even before having the doctor's appointment, because we felt so strongly that a life is a life, no matter how small. We wanted our little one to be celebrated, and this was a huge secret to not tell anyone! Remember how I mentioned earlier I'm not very patient?!

Arriving at our first ultrasound felt surreal. Jeremy was to my right, and my mom was to my left.

I diligently filled out the paperwork, and waited for my name to be called. Moments later I found myself sitting on the table and staring at the stirrups. The doctor came in, introduced himself, and spoke briefly before performing the sonogram.

Seeing our baby for the first time was overwhelming. I looked at the screen and at the tiny little bean and the tears began to fall. How miraculous! It was real. It was still too early to see the heartbeat and know the gender, but I felt from the beginning we were going to have a boy, so I started using male pronouns from then on.

We scheduled my eight-week appointment that day, the one where you get to hear the heartbeat and as we walked out of the office, we hit 'post' to let the world know we were expecting. It was the best kept secret of all time, and the amount of love we received was overwhelming.

I don't remember when exactly the paralyzing fear began, but I do know that around eight and a half weeks in, I felt like I could hardly breathe most of the time. With each moment that passed by my anxiety went through the roof. I had never dealt with anxiety like this before. I didn't want to say anything because I felt terrible that I was living in such fear. The fear that crippled me the most was wondering if I was going to lose him. Was it safe to get attached? To start dreaming of nursery ideas? To buy gender neutral clothes? Questions with no definitive answers. I was in such a dark place that my desire to look pregnant to prove that I was really having a baby ended with me gaining close to ten pounds in a couple weeks.

The statistics of miscarriage kept replaying over and over in my mind like a video that I couldn't turn off. I spent hours at work googling statistics and distancing myself from the baby growing inside of me. I felt so far from God during these weeks. I didn't trust Him. Heck, I didn't trust myself. It was unchartered territory, this struggle with my faith. I even felt guilty that I felt this way. I wanted to be alone, and eat. My purest form of self-care.

One day during my drive home from work I turned on the *We Will Not Be Shaken* album by Bethel Music. It had just been released a few months prior and one of the songs "No Longer Slaves" had been on repeat in my car. The bridge of the song had become my battle cry:

"You split the sea so I could walk right through it
You drown my fears in perfect love
You rescued me so I can stand and sing,
I am a child of God."

I needed all the fears that encompassed my pregnancy to be drowned in His perfect love. The God that knit me together and formed me in my mother's womb knew every single detail of my life before I was even born. He knew, and I needed to trust that ultimately, His plan would reign supreme.

The Sunday before Easter I spent some time at the feet of Jesus. I cried out to Him, and asked that His perfect will would be done in my life, and in our baby's. I was 10 ½ weeks along at this point, and was almost in the second trimester, which meant my risk of having a miscarriage would go down drastically. I felt lighter as I left church that day, and was filled with a hope I hadn't felt the entire pregnancy.

The next Sunday I was on the worship team for Easter. I was leading the song "Forever" by Kari Jobe and had been practicing it for weeks. The first and second services flew by, and we were in the middle of our third service when I had stepped out to use the restroom before going back up at the end. There, in the middle stall in the bathroom, I saw it. Blood.

PANIC

I stood there, stunned at the sight of bright red. I hadn't so much as spotted during the previous 11 ½ weeks, so I wasn't sure what to do. I walked out of the restroom and found my Jeremy. We had a bit of time left before needing to be back on stage so I rushed to call my on-call doctor and ask what we should do. Since it was a Sunday, and not just any Sunday, but Easter, it took a while to hear anything back. I should've known when I received the call back from the office that my experience with them was going to create more heartache than I could've ever imagined.

Against our doctor's suggestion, we decided that we would go to the Emergency Room and get things checked out. I wasn't in any pain, but there was still blood. We called my mom and dad on our drive to the hospital and as we hung up, I turned on worship music. I needed the worship music to help calm my spirit as we drove to the unknown. Although only a few miles away, it felt like the drive from the church to the hospital took an eternity. The song that was playing as we pulled into the ER was "It is well." I checked in, was triaged, and told to have a seat.

Two and a half hours later I was finally called back. I was advised to put on a gown, as the nature of the visit would require an ultrasound, and so I obeyed. After the ER doctor came in, he ordered the ultrasound and told me that hospital protocol states no one other than the patient is allowed in the room during the exam. I was wheeled into the room and had a sweet Ultrasound Technician waiting for me. She spoke sweetly, and told me no matter what, I was going to be ok. While the screen was turned away from me, when she turned the microphone on and no sound appeared, I knew. He was gone.

I was taken back to my room where Jeremy and my mom had patiently waited. My mom had left the room briefly to meet my dad in the waiting room, and not a moment later, the doctor came in. Divine timing is what I like to call it now. His demeanor had changed drastically, and he was very matter of fact. While I was 11, almost 12 weeks along, our baby, Everett Finn, was only measuring at 7 weeks, and there was no heartbeat. I was miscarrying.

NUMB

The tears from both Jeremy and me had progressed into full on weeps as my mom reentered the room. One look and a shake of my head was all it took. She knew. And we all lost it. My greatest fear, losing Everett, had just come to light.

We left the hospital completely different people. The next few hours went like a blur. We got back to our apartment and cried until morning.

My mind couldn't comprehend all that was going on. I was still pregnant, but this baby wouldn't survive. I was a parent, yet I would never hold my child. The toll it took on my body physically over the next 48 hours would lead me back to the hospital. It was traumatic.

As Jeremy and I had mentioned being pregnant so early to our family and friends, we knew we couldn't simply delete everything we had shared publicly and never talk about it again. So, I wrote and shared with the world our heartache as we were losing Everett. The outpouring of love, prayers, messages, food, flowers, and company was more than I could handle.

I kept writing because it helped me process through the pain, and I kept the worship music playing loudly, so as to drown out my own darkening thoughts. In the weeks following, my anger, resentment, and bitterness worsened. On paper, I had done everything right. I fell in love, got married, and then tried for a baby after saving myself for marriage.

I had always wanted to be a mom, and couldn't understand why others had their babies so easily and I didn't. It became an extremely dark season. Comments from those around me that were meant to bring comfort, only brought more anger and sorrow. For the record, while we may know that "God has a plan" and "it just wasn't meant to be," it doesn't mean we want to hear those phrases in our darkest moments. All I really wanted was for someone to say that they were sorry, and it totally sucked. Because let's face it. It did.

Jeremy and I tried to grieve together, and apart, in whatever way we could. Through a series of unfortunate events, six weeks after our loss, Jeremy lost his job and we had to move in with my parents. We weren't sure what life looked like. We had talked about selling everything and moving overseas, unsure of if or when we'd try for another baby. God had other plans for us though, as five and a half months after losing Everett, we found out we were pregnant again. I couldn't believe it. The trauma of my miscarriage had left me with some PTSD, and the minute the test strip turned pink I felt the fear rise up in me.

My pregnancy was unconventional. After breezing through the first trimester and into the second, we found out we were having a girl. It was one of the happiest days of our lives. She was growing beautifully, and showed no signs of any abnormalities. While everything looked good on paper, it didn't change the fact that every time I went to the bathroom,

I prayed I wouldn't see blood. And if you've been pregnant before, you know that's a lot of bathroom visits. I fought the battle between faith and fear, and had scriptures plastered everywhere. The one that I learned and recited more than any, was Philippians 4:6-7.

> *"Do not be anxious about anything, but in everything by prayer and supplication with thanksgiving let your requests be made known to God. And the peace of God, which surpasses all understanding, will guard your hearts and your minds in Christ Jesus."*

At 27 weeks and 5 days I was admitted to the hospital after finding out I had a high leak, causing Preterm Premature Rupture of the membranes. Basically, the amniotic fluid had started coming out, putting Maizie, and myself in distress, and at high risk of infection. The doctor put me on strict bedrest and had Maizie monitored 3 times daily. The goal was to make it to 34 weeks exactly. No one thought I would. The time spent in the hospital turned out to be the most peaceful I had felt in over a year. I used the days to journal, and spend time in the Word. I fought my way back to my faith and allowed the Lord's peace and presence to wash over me. The nurses had commented at one point about how different my room felt, how hopeful, and I beamed when I told them about how God had worked this all out. He knew in order for me to fight the fear of the enemy, we needed time together, and so this was how it happened.

At 34 weeks on the day, I delivered a tiny, 4lb. 15oz. baby, Maizie Jewell. After a 16-day stint in the NICU, we were sent home.

Throughout my entire pregnancy, miscarriage, and depression journey, God was constant. While I waivered, He did not. While I questioned, His answers never changed. While I pictured an ending that looked vastly different, His plan reigned supreme, and I can't imagine my life any other way.

THE MISSING COUPLE

SHARON BURCHAM

Several years ago, in our church choir, there was a young woman who always seemed to avoid me. One evening we were hosting an event at our house for the choir, and I asked if she and her family were coming . . . and she replied, "Absolutely not." A few hours later, much to my surprise, she was standing in our home amidst 75 other people. Gathering my courage, I asked her if we could speak privately. (I had to know what I had done to make her dislike me.) I was surprised and saddened to learn she didn't like me because she thought I had a perfect life.

Thinking back about those days, my life was good, and I didn't have to pretend. But for the past several years, I have had to pretend. After all, who wants people to know their life is a train wreck? Over the past several years, I have thought about that young woman who didn't like me. Maybe she is reading this story and will come away with a different opinion of me, because my life certainly has not been perfect.

My childhood was anything but ideal, so I clung to the fact that one day I would be "in charge" of my own life and it would look different. I am a person of faith and trusting God has been my mindset since I was 15 years old. Through challenges and hard times, I've been steadfast and in love with Jesus—so I was not easily rocked.

When I married my husband—who is a strong man of faith—I felt so secure in every way. He was my rock and I couldn't imagine anything changing my trust in him. We were happy. We both worked hard, and we were active in our church. We had amazing friends and spent lots of time with our daughter and two grandsons. So, while it wasn't perfect, we had carved out a nice life, with not too many worries.

Does life happen when we are not looking, or do we not look at our life because we don't want to see what's going on? Either way, I became an ostrich with my head in the sand.

For several years my husband and the life we loved gradually went away. It started with the loss of his career—not due to his fault. Then, an unexpected diagnosis for him that was troubling and painful. That was followed by a serious car accident he was in, the loss of a close friend of his, and the last blow was his diagnosis of throat cancer. That's a lot to deal with for anyone. He started coping by drinking.

Giving you a little back story, I have hated alcohol my

whole life. When I was a young girl, I endured some horrific experiences at the hands of someone who drank. My grasp of alcohol is simplistic. It makes people change. They can get angry or violent, act silly, do dumb things, and say things they shouldn't—or be someone they are not. Furthermore, they may or may not remember their behavior once they are sober. Now some people are okay with that, but not me. My entire life I have stayed away from alcohol. I just have never liked to be around it.

I'm very sure that my husband didn't start out to hurt me. His dependency on alcohol was a slow winding road going downward. A casual glass of wine with dinner or a beer on the golf course became "normal" for him. He began to acquire new friends. He moved from wine to vodka, and from drinking when out of our home to hiding it when in our home.

These changes happened over a few years. At first—I was angry, then sad, then back to angry, and I always pretended it wasn't happening. There were so many fights, and I cried so many tears. I didn't understand what a powerful addiction alcohol has on people.

In reality, alcohol had replaced most things and people in my husband's life. Family, church, vacations, and things we once did together—I now did alone. We lived in the same house, but there was no communication. I quit trying to make a difference, and he just wanted to be left alone to drink. I would constantly make excuses why he wasn't with me. Often, he would tell me he was sick or just not feeling well, and because of all the health challenges he had experienced, I chose to believe him for a long time. But eventually, I had to come to grips with what was happening. When I finally realized how much he was drinking, I was shocked. Of course, he was sick—he was drinking himself to death.

My life was barely tolerable, but I kept it all together on the outside. There were a handful of people who knew what was going on, and I am very grateful for their presence and their prayers in my life. Alcohol was robbing me of my wonderful husband, and he was letting it . . . but so was I. I had long conversations crying out to God (and my dog listened in), as I grieved over my loss.

I finally reached a breaking point, or thought I had, anyway. I was not going to live like this anymore. He had a choice to make. I guess I thought it was simple, and maybe he did too. But there is nothing simple about addiction. There were rehabs and plans for a better life going forward. There were promises, and in fairness, he believed what he was telling me. Always after a time of sobriety, he would go right back to a lifestyle that he couldn't seem to break away from. It was a vicious cycle.

Right about the time I didn't think that things could get any worse, they did. At the height of his drinking I discovered that he found someone to drink with, and that someone validated his drinking and encouraged him to continue down this self-destructive path. When confronted he declared that the relationship meant nothing to him, and he would end it, only to return to her when he would start drinking again. It crushed me. It was a double blow. We all say, "Well if my husband cheated on me, I would do such and such . . ." But would you? The emotions of mad and sad are very different. Mad makes us act on impulses; I had never been impulsive. I think before I act—at least usually. Our life had become such a lie—in all areas. And now to have to contend with another woman (regardless of his feelings toward her) devastated me yet again. He lied to me. He lied to himself and then I lied to myself, along with to everyone else. I still was not sharing with most family and friends because I felt so stupid. I didn't want to be the clueless person who didn't know what was happening in front of her. And, too, I didn't want my husband to be embarrassed that this is what his life had become. My protection of the situation only made things worse. I learned that I, too, had a capacity to deny, and I wasn't drinking.

Only in the movies you hear statements like: "Love means never having to say you're sorry" or "It would be a privilege to have my heart broken by you." Seriously, who says that?

My husband and I kept dancing with the issues. His deception to me was so painful. I didn't know what to do, so I did nothing, and lived in a sort of hell for a time. Not understanding addiction was one of my problems. The addict doesn't acknowledge the problem, and the family tries to help without knowing how. It reminds me of a hamster running on those little Ferris wheels in the cage—going 'round and 'round but never getting anywhere. After dealing with the truth of the situation for a few years, I came to this conclusion—to end the marriage. I knew my husband was a good man. I never had stopped believing that, but he was a good man who had lost his way. How had it happened? What could I have done differently? I didn't know, except I was tired of being hurt.

My husband desperately wanted another chance to make it right. He was sorry, but being sorry doesn't change anything. I had no more forgiveness to give, and I was all out of hope.

While in the process of making decisions about my life alone, our daughter asked if I would give my husband a six-month grace period if he met certain conditions. Reluctantly, I said I would, but I did not think he would be able to meet the conditions. He was, after all, an addict, and his life now revolved around alcohol. Ah, but she was smart, and as she laid out the conditions for him, I remember thinking, "Don't get too excited, Sharon, just take it one day at a time." I was truly ready at that point to let go. I was also so angry. I have never been an angry person. I just walk away and let everyone else fight. For the first time in my life my anger was off the charts. It was more like rage, and I had never had it before.

Now maybe because I kept everything bottled up for so long, it had to come out. I don't know. I didn't like it, and I didn't like him, and I wasn't very happy with me either.

It didn't take me too long to realize that my perspective had to change, regardless if we stayed together or not. Anger and bitterness will destroy you, and I had lost enough without losing myself too. I began to pray and study about grace. Max Lucado, one of my favorite authors, says that giving grace "allows us to speak honestly with words that are direct, but that are also strategically tucked inside an envelope of grace."

I asked myself not only "how," but "why" should I forgive my husband? I needed to approach the situation with my husband with grace because of all the grace I had received in my life. But the question remained in my heart, "How could I ever get over this feeling of being deceived?" Nelson Mandela said, "Forgiveness liberates the soul and removes fear."

I became quiet before the Lord. What would it cost me to give my husband grace? How would life change for me if I started applying grace instead of hostility to our broken marriage, to my life, to my husband's life? John Ortberg's book, *Soul Keeping*, was transformational for me. A quote that stuck out to me was: "The world diverts my soul attention when it encourages me to think of myself more as a victim than as a human. I am so wrapped up in the hurt I have received that I do not notice the hurt I inflict." It rammed my heart.

The second thing I did was learn about the power of alcohol and the hold it can have on people. The phrase "recovering addict" is used instead of "recovered addict" because it's a choice the addict makes every day, one day at a time. The question is often asked, "How long have you been sober?" The answer, just as often, comes back, "Just for today." I heard a man tell us he's been saying that for 30+ years. He made that choice today for today. That's what addicts have to do. It's not easy.

My husband and I started having long, honest conversations. There were lots of tears. I know it was hard for him to tell me all that he had gone through, and it was hard for me to hear it. I am a wall builder. So, when he would be talking, I would silently pray that I might have grace and not shut him out for telling me his feelings. You know, for years everything with me was always "fine." Do you do that? I think we all probably do to an extent, and then we laugh because we do it. I'm not suggesting you bare your soul to the Barista at Starbucks who innocently asks, "How are you?" But letting things stay bottled up and always being "fine" isn't the answer. I learned that the hard way. Looking back, I believe that if my husband had dealt with his disappointments up front instead of pretending to be "fine," he would not have turned to alcohol.

My husband started attending AA, and we both learned from it. My heart still hurt, Even So, I had to begin to forgive him in order to move forward. Regardless of where the marriage ended up, I knew that if I waited until I *felt* like forgiving him, it might never happen. Feelings are fickle, and they can change quickly. Forgiveness disarms the Enemy and changes perspective.

The infamous six-month mark came and went, and our home was less tense. There was no drinking; there were no fights, and there was a lot of truth telling. I began to understand that as much as I was hurting, my husband was hurting too. He had lost himself, just as much as I lost him. He was continuing to meet all the conditions though. And I was very proud *of* him and *for* him. Again, from *Soul Keeping,* John Ortberg says: "There is pain that means things are coming apart, but then sometimes there is pain that things might be able to come back together. Surgery can be as painful as stabbing, but it leads to healing."

There is a message in my mess. I strongly believe that God never wastes a hurt. God never wanted any of this to happen. You might ask: "Why didn't He stop it?" Because we have free will and we exercise it all the time. Even So, God was right there in our midst. My husband should have died in the car accident; he didn't. He should have died after his spleen ruptured and he lost 6 liters of his blood; he didn't. When his alcohol level was ridiculously high on admission to a rehab facility, he should have had seizures or blacked out, but he didn't. His recovery from throat cancer was so incredible that the oncologist stated, "He was living on the other side of miracle." I should have walked away from our marriage, but I didn't.

I have a life verse in the Bible. Its Jeremiah 29:11, "For I know the plans I have for you," says the Lord. "They are plans for good and not for disaster, to give you a future and a hope." I knew I needed to live and go forward with the knowledge that God has it all.

So you might want to know where the marriage is today. My Pastor recently said: "God will give a fresh blueprint when we seek Him. Some things need to be demolished, while others need to be reclaimed. He is our solid foundation." Think about that for just a moment. He – God – is my foundation. We lean on God's Grace. It's powerful; it's calming, and it's peaceful in the midst of a storm. In all of our lives there will be storms of one sort or the other. I have learned that I need to do a better job of dancing in those storms. If we could turn back the clock and approach things differently, would we? Yes, indeed we both would. But we can't go back. God is in the tensions; He can handle all our stuff, and He has anchored us. We pray for more Grace, more Love, and more Time to make better memories. We can't change yesterday, but we have today. One day at a time.

JAKE: THE RAILFAN MAN

TRICIA GLEGHORN

I had to park in the last row of the parking lot to join the mass of parents coming to the annual elementary school curriculum night. Simpson was a good school and parent participation was high. We all went through the two sets of double doors, filled the entry way to capacity and then headed to our respective classrooms to meet our student's teachers for the upcoming school year. The moment was poignant because it was at that moment I got a preview of what our future was going to look like – different. The crowd of parents had all turned into the hallway on the right to go to the lower grade classrooms, but I turned left to go towards the special education classrooms. There were hundreds of parents who turned right but when I got to my classroom there were three of us. The significance of it hit me as I turned left, and I sat on a bench in the hallway to compose myself before heading into the classroom.

Jacob is my precious 16-year-old boy. He loves trains. And when I say he loves trains, I mean he LOVES trains! Our family has spent over 100 hours on Amtrak; we have ridden trains in a dozen states and another half-dozen countries. We spend vacations chasing trains, are looking for a next home that is along the tracks, and spend at least 10 hours a week trackside.

My boy has autism. His fascination with trains is called a perseveration, and while it can be frustrating it is also one of the things I love about him. It makes him who he is, and his incredible passion for all things trains attracts people to him. It also showcases how smart he is when focused on a subject he cares about. The flipside is that this appetite to train watch is never satisfied. Jake could care less about the fact that dinner is almost ready, there is homework to be done, or other people may want to talk about something besides trains. As a family, we have decided to embrace this. We have made an intentional choice to be railfans (what people who make train watching a hobby call themselves). It creates a slice of life where we can interact with our child. We use train watching as an opportunity to travel, to learn new things, and to teach life lessons.

Our journey began early as milestones were not reached as a baby. Speech was very slow to come, and movement was severely delayed. I remember when my suspicions came together, and I knew I had to do something. Jake and I were at a friend's 1st birthday party, Jake was the oldest child there, and yet, he was clearly behind the other children developmentally. It had been great to spend an afternoon seeing friends and connecting with other moms, but I left that party knowing I had to do something for Jake. The pediatrician had told me there was a wide range of normal and not to worry just yet, but I knew it was time to take action.

Fifteen years ago autism awareness was not what it is now, and there were no highly publicized campaigns of what autism looks like in toddlers. I had no idea what to expect when I scheduled our first appointment with a specialist. I certainly had no idea that this was the beginning of an eight-year journey to get a diagnosis. This wasn't the type of thing I could go and get a prescription for and be with a week later.

The specialist did not have a diagnosis, but agreed that there were some red flags and that we needed to jump into therapy immediately. We started on a course of five therapies a week. It was incredibly hard. It was crazy trying to juggle schedules and budgets to make it happen, but by God's grace, we did. Thankfully family jumped in and helped in every way, and employers were gracious to allow flexible schedules and provide good insurance. I cannot help but have extreme gratefulness as I think about that season in our lives. I know it has helped make Jake as successful as he is today.

As I spent time working with the therapists and Jake it was easy to see how delayed he was. Jake was over two years old and could not roll a ball back and forth, which apparently mimics the give and take of conversation; he did not tolerate any touching of his face; he struggled with motor coordination and he had zero words. We were making some progress with motor skills, sensitivities and eating, but very little progress with speech.

These challenges played out in crazy real ways. Jake hated for his mouth to be touched so brushing teeth was an exhausting ordeal which required two adults and a very unhappy toddler. Transitioning from one place to another must have stressed poor Jake out, and so when I would arrive to pick him up, he would literally try to burrow himself into the corner of the room. I would eventually give up trying to coax him out of the corner and pick him up, screaming and kicking, and walk out of the building like that. People would stare at us as if I must have been hurting my child, or I just did not know how to control him.

The lack of speech was so frustrating. I wanted to know why Jake was mad. I wanted to be able to understand him (as much as anyone understands a toddler). He would incoherently get louder and louder, as if the problem were me not hearing him. He would glare at me with those beautiful big eyes, as if I were choosing to ignore what he was trying to communicate. I was trying so hard to listen, but could not understand. We used pictures and basic sign language, but it was a poor substitute.

Thankfully, at three years old we had a breakthrough. Hard to say if it was the coming together of 16 months of therapy, or if it was the addition of a new therapy, but after a few months of hippotherapy (equine therapy) Jacob began to speak. Within the next three months we went from minimal sounds to all of the sounds of the alphabet, to basic, but complete sentences.

The progress came just in time because Jacob's third birthday meant a lot of changes. The county program that supported our early intervention efforts ended at the age of three and support was now available only through an early intervention pre-school program. The therapy the school offered was not the quantity or quality that we had been receiving. We signed up for the preschool program and secured private therapy. On Jake's third birthday our cost for therapy went up over five times.

As I think about that season of life, I remember the financial stress, not getting near enough sleep, fear of what was behind these delays, discussions late into the night trying to figure out next steps, and many, many prayers. I remembered the first specialist we saw told us not to worry because 80% of kids grow out of their developmental delays by the time they are three. I spent time learning what was and wasn't typical at this age, and it was evident that Jake wasn't where his peers were. He was three, but there were no signs of growing out of this.

It was the beginning of endless doctor visits, issues with the school system, and testing at both school and doctors. My husband and I were both working full time and I honestly do not know how we did it. I do know that our employers and our family were incredibly generous and helpful. It was an odd season with friends. I would share my concerns and some would tell us to pray harder, and others assured us it was just a phase. They were well meaning, and just did not know how to deal with it. To be honest, neither did I, which also showed up in weird ways. One day at a church event, I ran into a friend I had not seen in a few months. She asked me how Jake was, and with no warning, I burst into tears. So random and so weird, but these days were a blur of action trying to solve a problem we had not even defined. It was as if something was over our heads and we knew it was big, but we did not know what it was. Truth be told, I was not ready to know.

After a few years of this, my husband and I decided to make the call to the developmental pediatrician (a pediatrician with both medical and psychological training). I had been told this is where we would likely get a diagnosis. The doctor agreed we were on the right track with our therapies, and the special education preschool. She said Jake had an obvious desire to be social and that she did not think he had autism, but she reserved the right to make that call later. She also had us run through a battery of other tests to rule out other conditions.

We continued our breakneck speed of life, getting therapies in, working full time, and juggling everything to pay for it, and were pleased to see progress. However, the second year of preschool was terrible and thus began the never-ending quest of trying to figure out what was going to be the best option for school.

School has been one of the most challenging aspects of this journey. We had academics to consider, whether we wanted Jake to have a chance to be with "typical peers" and the concern of how he would feel when he wasn't treated well or couldn't keep up. As public-school options did not seem to work well we tried private schools. We saw amazing social-emotional growth, but then the academics seemed to slide. We were paying thousands of dollars, driving two hours a day to get to school and not even knowing if it would result in a usable diploma.

The end of every school year would have me reevaluating what would be best for the next year, and second guessing whether we had made the right choice the previous year. We knew there were trade-offs, but wanted to make sure we were on the right side of those trade-offs. Was the debt worth it? Would he even be able to get a high school diploma? Would this give him the social skills needed to maintain a job, or the life skills to be independent? What was most important and how should we be prioritizing? These are hard questions to try to get out ahead of when your child is only nine years old.

Jake is going into 10th grade, and he has been to seven different schools in every setting we can think of. We have utilized all that public schools have to offer, and we have paid the high cost of the best, special education, private schools, and they have all had their positives and negatives.

Along the way, we finally did get a diagnosis that tells us that Jake is on the autism spectrum, has ADHD, and severe anxiety. He is verbal and high functioning. We are blessed and we are challenged.

I began to wrestle with how perspective plays into this. On one hand, I was sad as I had to admit the real difficulties that would be a part of Jake's life for the rest of his life, and how it would impact our hopes and dreams for him. On the other hand, I felt guilty because I knew I had it "better" than some of my friends whose children needed an incredible amount of care to get through every single day, and whose lives were much more precarious. I choose to be grateful and focus on the positive. I realize so many people have much more significant challenges than we do, and yet the reality is that our lives are not easy. When I gloss over the difficulties and don't acknowledge them, I diminish God's grace in a journey that cries out for His wisdom, strength and provision.

Every single day is impacted by the reality of raising a child who sees the world differently than we do. Some days we see progress like an understanding of someone else's perspective or a sweetness of heart that cares about someone else being sad and are encouraged. Today has been a battle because according to Jake I have, "exacting standards when it comes to showering" and by that he means that I want him to wash his hair and his face. Others days are frustrated by the single-minded insistence on his way for everything, homework that turns into an argument AGAIN, or when he won't eat dinner because of the grill marks on the burger. I get phone calls or texts 24 hours a day from him as his anxious spirit worries about everything from a train delay to a thunderstorm.

It is not what I expected, and I want so much for my son. I want him to know our love for him, and God's love for him. I want him to have options for a job, to be safe, and to have friends. I want people to treat him well and not take advantage of him. I want him to have as much independence as he wants. I want people to see past the quirks to see the beautiful young man he is. I wish I could somehow work hard enough to guarantee these things for him. I would make that trade in a moment! We would be willing to be perpetually exhausted and broke if we could somehow be assured he would have these things.

Reality is that the journey continues with no outcome being guaranteed. Looking back, I see 16 years of raising a child with autism as an unexpected journey that has had more twists and turns than I could have imagined. I see a lot of tired days, fear of the unknown, thankfulness for my strong husband, and God's faithfulness. Looking forward, I try to find the balance between being proactive and preparing my son to live a fulfilling life and not thinking too much about it because the stats, the unknowns and the fear can easily be overwhelming.

I choose to focus on the truth that God has gifted me with a precious son who makes me smile. One of my prayers for Jake, from his very first days, has been that God would bless him and allow him to be a blessing to others. Even though Jake is only 16, it is clear God is answering my prayer. His enthusiasm and passion are energizing, his expressive admiration for people who do jobs he likes remind us not to take people for granted. His true curiosity causes people to smile as he genuinely cares about what they do, and his appreciation is sincere. He thanks the trash collectors and claps for them when they come by; he thanks police and firefighters for their service, and tells the janitors how much he appreciates them for keeping his school clean. He knows how to bless others!

Friends, I know you have difficulties of your own. It is my prayer that my story encourages you. The same God who has been faithful to teach me amidst the struggles and to provide for us every step of the way is available to you and whatever challenges you face. My story is born from my experience, but we all have a story and the good and bad provide opportunities for us to see God at work and allow Him to show His faithfulness. I am so very aware that many of your stories are full of pain and hurt that I do not understand, but what I do know is that God is big enough to walk with each and every one of us wherever we are.

I adore my son and I love him very much. I appreciate his passion, his focus, and his directness, but his disability presents challenge after challenge for him. I see God give him the grit to move forward and I am grateful. I see God provide wonderful friends, family, teachers, and caregivers to make life better for him, and I am so grateful. Still…in my perfect world he would not have to struggle with autism, and I would not have to struggle with fear of the future for him.

We adore this young man God has given us and yet we acknowledge raising a child with autism is hard. It is expensive, it is exhausting, it is nerve wracking. ***Even So***…God is enough! He has provided me with Truth after Truth to tell me who He is and how much He loves my son. God has given us so many victories. Jake just finished his first year of high school at a public school and he LOVED it. He was on student council, a part of the rugby team, and may get a high school diploma. I am grateful and yet I am realistic enough to know that I have no idea how this next semester will go. Matt Redman's song, "Never Once" sums it up perfectly. It speaks to the hope I have as we face an uncertain future, and so, I would love to end my chapter sharing this reminder of God's great faithfulness with you.

Standing on this mountaintop

Looking just how far we've come

Knowing that for every step

You were with us

Kneeling on this battle ground

Seeing just how much You've done

Knowing every victory

Was Your power in us

Scars and struggles on the way

But with joy our hearts can say

Yes, our hearts can say

Never once did we ever walk alone

Never once did You leave us on our own

You are faithful, God, You are faithful.

Matt Redman – *"Never Once"*

TRUST THE PROCESS

VICKIE HINTZ

By 1991 we had been married over sixteen years. We had stable jobs, served God faithfully and were raising two growing boys. To help you understand why we came to the decisions we made at that time, I want to take you back to where it all started.

We got married earlier than we should have with a child on the way. We went off to college at 17 and 18 years old with a three week old infant. Needless to say, we accumulated many school loans, but we had to have at least one of us with a degree. During this season we grew by leaps and bounds in our relationship with the Lord. We knew Jesus was our only hope to survive in marriage, raising kids and everyday life.

Five years later my husband graduated with a teaching degree in math and physics, with a healthy start toward a master's degree. Following graduation, he was offered a teaching job and we began a new phase in our lives. He taught school and I worked as an administrative assistant for the director of the local hospital. We were faithfully growing in our relationships with God and with each other, and we stayed busy raising our two growing sons. Life was a constant financial struggle due to how we began our adult years. This is how our story began and how God redeemed not just us, but our finances as well.

Needless to say, we will be forever grateful to our Almighty Father for always being there. As we gave our lives fully to Jesus, our Savior, God helped us mature in Him as well as in the natural. He was ever faithful to teach us as we went through life. We often say, "Where would we be without God?" He forgives our sins, picks us up when we fall down, encourages us when we doubt and never, ever leaves us. The following paragraphs are a testament to all of this.

We had been living in Minot, North Dakota for eight years. I worked at our church as the administrative assistant. My husband taught seventh grade math, coached football and basketball, and painted houses during the summer. None of these jobs brought in much money. Life was not easy. During that time we became weary from the constant financial struggle. As we processed this with my sister and her family who lived in Indiana and with dear friends of ours who lived in Iowa, both were encouraging us to come live near them. Due to these connections and after praying about it, we began a job search in both places. Through that search my husband was offered a job in Des Moines, Iowa.

It was June of 1991 as we said goodbye to our family in North Dakota, our home state. The truck was packed, and the car was loaded down as we headed to Iowa. This move was going to give us a better life. Our boys were going to be a senior and a freshman; it was not a great time to move our family, but we were quite desperate for a better life. So, after much prayer, on to Iowa we went.

We were in Iowa a matter of a few weeks and realized that my husband's job was more stressful than we anticipated. The dollars were even tighter than we predicted due to a cost of living increase. We did not have internet access like today, so we were not as prepared for this move as we should have been. *Even So*, we still had hope that this was an overall good decision. Two weeks later, we were there a total six weeks, my husband ended up in the emergency room because the doctor thought he was having a heart attack. After a night of testing they concluded that it was stress. At this time all of us were working, doing what we could to get by, including our boys delivering daily papers. So much for a better life and less stress.

During that first month there, we found a wonderful church and it became our support group. Our boys were enjoying the youth group. Our oldest son, who is an extrovert quickly became very involved. Because of his involvement, before we left the emergency room, church people were there praying and supporting us. One of God's many blessings.

Following that experience, we had to move on with life. It was time to make this area our home. Hard or not, God was still our rock. It was time to find a house.

We picked the suburb that had the high school where we wanted our boys to graduate. We found a home that we could afford which was a fixer upper. We purchased a fixer upper before it was a popular idea, but over time we made it our home. Yes, we lived in it as we worked on it. Yea, that was a lot of fun in the midst of being financially tight. No, not really...

Fall came, our boys were in school and we were living in our fixer upper. Money was as tight as could be, so the fixer upper plans were put on hold and we made do with what we had. In the middle of all this we learned to trust God and to grow and to mature in His word. As I look back, God was always faithful to provide, it just did not look the way I thought it should look.

Through our uncomfortableness God taught us valuable lessons that were life changing. We spent more time on our knees leaning on God because where else could we go? He was our only hope. Sunday morning messages seemed to be directed at us in such a way that we joked that our pastor was watching us through our windows. But, that is exactly how our awesome almighty God works. He is ever present in all circumstances. And, He sure was for us. Slowly finances began loosening up. Job promotions and changes helped us finally fix up our sweet little home. We added a bathroom, painted kitchen cabinets, painted appliances, tore down wallpaper, and replaced carpets. Mind you, monies were still tight so we did all this work ourselves trying to save every penny we could. But again, God was in it all. He found us bargains, kept our appliances working, and brought true contentment to our hearts.

After living there three years we decided it was time to upgrade to another home in which we again could add some changes, bringing more value to the home as well as giving us more room. Our sweet little home on Chapel Drive sold quickly, and we moved November of 1994 into a home with more potential. Yes, there was more carpet to change, wallpaper to tear down and a bedroom and bathroom to add to the lower level. We had our work cut out for us, but now we had experience, and it looked more like an opportunity than a 'have to' decision.

Our youngest son was a high school senior, and our oldest was back home from college for a season. (Another story for another time.) We all had jobs and life was moving along. We made it through Christmas and into springtime, which is generally my favorite time of the year, that is until 1995. It was the beginning of March, and my husband came by the CPA firm, where I worked to inform me, he was among 65 people that were downsized. To say I was this strong woman of faith, at this point of the story, would be a lie. I worked for a wonderful Christian man. He not only encouraged us, but he gave us some wise counsel.

Following this turn of events I went home and sat in a chair crying. All I could think of was, oh no, here we go again. We were just starting to get ahead of things and this happens. As I was sitting there crying and sort of praying; no, just crying, our oldest son came in the room and confronted me... He looked at me and said "Mom, do you believe in God and His Word?" Of course, through my tears, I said, "Yes." But, I will be honest, I was not looking forward to another season of pinching every penny we had while working our bottoms off just to get by again! Following a dialogue with my son, God reminded me what He had me reading every morning for the last few months. I got my Bible and opened it to Psalms 112.

This beautiful Psalms was my lifeline during those times. I know it is a little long, but these words ministered to me and I hung onto them for dear life. "Praise the LORD! Blessed is the man who fears the LORD, Who delights greatly in His commandments. His descendants will be mighty on earth; the generation of the upright will be blessed. Wealth and riches will be in his house, and his righteousness endures forever. Unto the upright there arises light in the darkness; He is gracious, and full of compassion, and righteous. A good man deals graciously and lends; He will guide his affairs with discretion. Surely, he will never be shaken; the righteous will be in everlasting remembrance. He will not be afraid of evil tidings; His heart is steadfast, trusting in the LORD. His heart is established; He will not be afraid, until he sees his desire upon his enemies. He has dispersed abroad, He has given to the poor; His righteousness endures forever; His horn will be exalted with honor." Psalms 112:1-9 NKJV

As I mentioned above, these words carried me through those days. They addressed every concern I had. Verse 2 - He promised to take care of my descendants. Verses 3 - Our needs will be met. Verse 5 and 6 - He guides us and we will not be shaken. Again, glory be to our God who so graciously prepared me for this season of life.

My husband knocked on every door in the metro area, and no job opened up for him. He was working with a headhunter as well. We knew we did not want to leave the area, but we wanted God's will for our life, and we needed my husband to be employed. Remember, we really loved our church and where we lived. Our prayer was, please God open a door in the Des Moines area.

July came and our youngest had graduated high school, I was working two jobs and my husband was working odd jobs and searching for full time employment. Then we received a call from the head hunter and he had a potential job in Minneapolis. We had no desire to move further north than where we were. But, as I stated earlier, we needed employment, and we wanted God's will. The job offer came through and we made plans to move to Minnesota. Really God, really? We rejoiced that God provided. But, we still questioned this offer because it just was not how we wanted it. Our desire was to one day move south, not further north.

My husband accepted the job on a Friday. We had been living in this current home eight months and were still renovating the lower level. We could not afford a realtor as we had no equity in this home. So, God what do we do? Remember Psalms 112? Verse one says, "Blessed is the man who fears the Lord." Let me tell you, when God says it, it is true!

The Sunday following the acceptance of the Minnesota employment we went to church as any normal Sunday. We were so blessed to have employment that my sweet husband wept through the whole church service. He was so relieved and so grateful to God that he was overwhelmed with God's goodness. I, on the other hand, was exhausted as I had worked all night at a previous job I had had. By the time we went to church I had been up 24 hours.

After church, I went to bed and my husband was praying about the house. How do we sell a house with no equity? What he did know was that he needed to finish our projects. So, he was on his way to Walmart to get supplies to work on our downstairs. During that trip, God told him to stop at an open house. He argued with God. Why go to an open house when we have a house to sell? Well, once again God had a plan. Because my husband was obedient, he ran into someone at the open house that we knew. He told her our story and she said she was looking to buy a house in the area. She asked to come see it that afternoon. She saw every room but the one where I was sleeping. Two days later she offered us full price. God sold our house without a realtor or a for sale sign in the yard. Again, our awesome God took care of us. Then it was time for the appraisal. We were nervous because we were finishing our downstairs on weekends, and we did not know how he would appraise the house in its current state. I am not exaggerating here, my son can attest to this fact. Before the appraiser left he says to our son and myself: "I don't usually do this, but I felt so impressed to say that God wants you to know He is in this move." Once again, after the appraiser left, I sat in the same chair and cried. This time in total awe of our Almighty, All-Sufficient God!

When my husband got downsized, we had a house that we had owned for eight months, two older vehicles with payments and a son who had just graduated high school. *Even So*, when we left Iowa the first weekend in August, the house was sold, and we had enough money to pay off both vehicles and to make a down payment on a house in Minnesota. How does that happen, considering our situation? There is only one answer. God!

On a side note, that move set us up for an employment opportunity a couple of years later that completely freed our finances. Our oldest son, the one who challenged my tears, is pastoring and has for years now. As I sit here putting my thoughts to print, I marvel at God's plans over our lives. And now 25 years later as I write this, we have built a house in that same area as God has moved us back. Why have we moved back, you ask? One reason is because we have a son, daughter-in-law, and two wonderful grandsons here. Time will tell if God has more reason than that. What I do know is that I feel like I am back home.

I sit here writing this and I am overwhelmed once again by the goodness of our big and wonderful God. He did not promise a rose garden, but He said He will never leave us no matter what comes our way.

EVERYONE HAS A STORY

TIFFANY SKIPPER

Everyone has a story; I have a story! My life has been full of ups and downs, twists and turns, good and bad. There are parts of my story I wish I could change, and there are parts of my story I wouldn't trade for anything. My story includes failures and victories, lessons learned, and some details I choose to forget. Through it all, my God has been faithful. He has been there with me and has pulled me through.

I was in a funky place not too long ago. You know what I'm talking about, one of those wonderful pity-party moments, not the fun party where there is cake. I love cake! But there was no cake at this party, it was just me, myself, and I sitting in a pit. It actually turned out to be a pivotal moment in my life. I was reading the Book of Numbers (yes, really Numbers). If I›m honest, it has never been one of my favorite books of the Bible. My daily reading plan said the Book of Numbers was where I was supposed to be, but my heart was not excited as I picked up my Bible. I just wanted to read it quickly and check the box off that I had read my Bible that day. God had another plan in store for me as I began reading. There was a simple verse that stuck out to me and truly has changed my heart and my outlook on some things and circumstances that I face.

Now let me set this up for you. The Israelites were in the wilderness wandering around. They had seen some pretty amazing miracles of God, and God had been providing for them every day and leading them, yet they still managed to complain about what He was doing for them. Think about it, they had seen Him part the Red Sea, give them water from a rock, lead them with a pillar of fire by night and a pillar of cloud by day, and so much more. At this particular part of the story they started to have cravings for things they weren't having any more, like meat! God had been providing manna (which was this special bread from heaven), but they were sick of it and wanted something more. So here comes the verse.... (*now when you read it read it, in your best complaining voice, it just sounds better!*)

> **Numbers 11:4-6 "This added to the discontentment of the people of Israel and they wept, "Oh, for a few bites of meat! Oh that we had some of the delicious fish we enjoyed so much**

in Egypt, and the wonderful cucumbers, and melons, leeks, onions and garlic! But now our strength is gone, and day after day we have to face this Manna!"

I know you are asking, "Really...this verse changed her life?" Well, I thought the same thing when I read it, but then I felt the Holy Spirit say to me, "That sounds just like you!" And I'm thinking, it doesn't sound like me at all. I would never complain and say, "Oh that I had cucumbers and leeks and garlic!" Now if it said, "Oh that I had chocolate cake and salty French fries and ice cream, then yes, but God that doesn't sound like me at all. I would never cry out for leeks and garlic!" Then I had this moment where I felt the Holy Spirit say, "But yes, it does sound like you, you are not satisfied with the way I have been providing for you. You have been complaining and not grateful."

WOW! I had a moment with the Lord that brought me to my knees. I thought of all the moments I asked the question "Why?"

> Why is this happening to me?
> Why can't I have the victory in this area of my life?
> Why am I having to face this trial?
> And so many more "Why?" questions...

Maybe you've had some "Whys."

> Why is my marriage falling apart?
> Why am I sick? Why is my child sick?
> Why did my loved one have to die?
> Why do I have to put up with that?
> Why? Why? Why?

"Why can't we just have meat?" Sounds a little familiar now, doesn't it?

I could go on and on with the "Why" questions. The awesome thing about God is He can handle our questions. In all likelihood we may never know the answer to the "Whys." However, it was in this moment I really felt the Holy Spirit tell me I was asking the wrong question. Maybe, just maybe, rather than ask "Why," we should ask this question, "God, how will you show your glory?"

Let me explain, in John 9 Jesus had an encounter with a blind man. The disciples asked him a question, "Why was this man born blind? Was it a result of his sins or that of his parents?" Even the disciples asked "Why?" Just like us, they want to know why do bad things happen to good people? Why? Jesus' answer is so beautiful and I believe it shows us His heart. He says to them in verse 3, "Neither, but it is to bring God glory." Then Jesus spits on the ground, makes a mud pie, puts it on the man's eyes, and tells him to go wash them off, and he is healed! Amazing! A beautiful story of healing and restoration. If we think about it, Jesus teaches us so much in this encounter. It's a simple, yet beautiful lesson.... The "Why" doesn't matter, it's all about the glory.

God, how will you get the glory in this situation? What if we started asking that question? What if we chose not to ask "Why?" But we looked at the mountain in front of us and said, "God, how are you going to get the glory?" We must never forget the enemy will always come against anything that brings God glory (you, your life, your marriage, your family). But our amazing, sovereign God doesn't waste anything! In every part of your story, especially the messiest parts, He is working it all for good to accomplish His plan. (Romans 8:28). God is always working, and He isn't finished working on you until you see Him one day face to face. He's not giving up on you, so don't give up on Him!

Try this... Change your question from "Why" to "How will you get the Glory in this mess, God?" Then let Him start to show you, teach you, and make you into a powerful woman of God He has called you to be. Understand, in no way, am I saying this is easy; it's actually one of the hardest things you will do, but it's so worth it! If we allow him, He takes us through whatever trial we are facing, and He makes us stronger and more like Him. Why? For His glory!

As you read these stories, you can see the beautiful thread of God's love and grace flowing through all of these ladies' lives. While each story is unique and each outcome looks dif-

ferent there is something that resonates in each...***Even So***...
GOD!!!! You can see how God took the mess and created
a beautiful story for His glory! When you get on the other
side of the story, you see the answer to your "Why," It was
for His glory all along.

Oh the beauty of our God if we allow Him into our story.
The ***Even So*** that He moves mountains and sets captives free
and brings joy unspeakable and hope that doesn't disappoint!
He ushers in a peace that doesn't make sense. He remains
faithful, even when we walk away from Him. We just have
to make the choice to allow Him to come into our messy
stories, because He has an ***Even So*** for everyone.

This is the truth.... sometimes life is messy, actually a
lot of times life is messy. We are just human after all. He is
GOD, the creator of the universe, the one who set the stars
into place; He is the one who told the oceans where to stop
and the land to start; He is the one who created all things,
even you! He knows every little detail about you. He knows
how to get us out of the mess, that in some ways and sometimes, we have created ourselves. And when we, who are His
daughters, His creation, lean into Him and trust in Him, He
shows up. Even though it doesn't make sense, and even when
He doesn't operate in our perfect timing, He is right on time.
Somehow, someway, He is on time. It's crazy, it's perfect, and
it's amazing!

Let me say it this way. Remember after Jesus was born
there was a King named Herod, and there were three wise

men who were following the star. The King expected them to report back to him. When they didn't, King Herod was angry and worried that a new king could come and take his place so he sent word to have all the babies under two years of age killed. Horrible story, I know, but the thing we forget so often was that this didn't take God by surprise. He knew the enemy would create a horrible plan to take His son out, and He knew the enemy would go to any extreme to take out the plan of God.

The enemy planned to take out the promised child.... *Even So* God made a way! God woke Joseph up and told him to flee to Egypt so the child would be safe. And we know the rest of the story, Jesus grows up and saves us all!! So what's the point in me telling you this? Well I'll tell you...God is always one step ahead of the enemy. God always has a plan. We just have to choose to listen to His plan and trust it. The enemy has a plan for your life as well. It's to steal, kill, and destroy. The enemy wants to take you out, to take your marriage out, to take your family, your hope, your faith. He wants to plant fear and worry and anxiety in your heart and to ultimately keep you from living a life that is free and full because of what God has done for you.

The good news is God has a plan for you too, and His plan is beautiful. It's attached to His purpose and His destiny over your life. The point is to lean into God's presence and allow him to walk you through every moment of your life.

He brings the beauty to the messy parts. Why? So He can get the glory!

Don't ever forget that our God always wins. I am actually a very competitive person and I don't ever want to be on the losing team so I can talk smack to the enemy and tell him where to go…if you know what I mean. I put him in his place because he has no authority over me. I also have to make the choice to allow God in fully, so He can move mountains and make the impossible possible.

God's word ways, "If He said it, He will do it." Your story, no matter how messy it is, God already has an *Even So* prepared for you. That is crazy good news. Let me say that again….Your story, no matter how messy it is, God already has an *Even So* prepared for you! His word is so full of promises, thousands of them. Grab one of them and hold onto it. Stand in the promise that God is faithful, and He will show up and show off in your life.

Each of us has a story. Our stories are different, yet they are the same, because we serve a God who works all things out for the good of those who are called to His purposes. Each story is a story of grace and love. Can you see the beautiful thread of grace and love woven through the family of God?

Through your life personally? That's the beauty of it, it's for everyone, yet it's personal, just for you.

If you don't believe it, read Hebrews 11… the chapter of the heroes of the faith. I love it. It encourages me. It helps me to know I am not alone in this thing; that's another reason we wrote this book together so you will know that you too are not alone. You have sisters in Christ who have been there, done that, and got the t-shirt! We have your back, and we are praying for you. Even now we pray God is speaking to you and bringing hope to you through these testimonies of God's glory.

Hebrews 11: 1-2 (NLT) "Faith shows the reality of what we hope for; it is the evidence of things we cannot see." Through their faith, the people in days of old earned a good reputation. Their names are in this chapter because of their reputation to trust God no matter what, because He is God and he is faithful.

Then it goes on and lists the names of all the heroes of the Bible. Each has as story. Each is a story woven with God's love and grace. Stories of having courage, of stepping out, of trust, of dreams, of standing alone, of leading, and even persecution. Then in verse 32 it says "How much more do I need to say? It would take too long to recount the stories of faith of…." It lists more names and their challenges and circumstances and how God never left them or forsaked them.

You see, everyone has a story, and God wants everyone to have a God story…an **Even So**! Don't you love that it says it would take too long to recount them all. Wow, just think about that for a minute and then add on all the faithful that have lived since then. God has been working and He still is working all the time; actually he is working nonstop to create *Even So* moments in the lives of His children. He is doing that even now for you because he loves you. Selah (it means that what was just said was pretty amazing and worthy to praise God for, think about that for a moment). Let me say it again. God is working out an *Even So* moment in your life right now because He loves you! Selah!

Then the chapter ends with Hebrews verse 39, "All these people earned a good reputation because of their faith, yet none of them received all that God had promised. For God had something better in mind for us, so that they would not reach perfection without us." Wait, what? They didn't receive all that was promised? That is not encouraging. Well, actually it is because the ALL that was promised was Jesus! And we now have Jesus. He is our everything; we will one day be with Him; we will be perfected in Him, and along with all who have gone before us because of Him. Such an awesome thought. So let your reputation (and I mean your reputation with God, most importantly) be one that is known because of righteousness, that you are a daughter of the King of Kings, and you are one of those people that believe God and take Him at His Word. Then watch God weave His love and grace though your life, because after all, you are His daughter and God loves to take care of His children.

Even So…God!